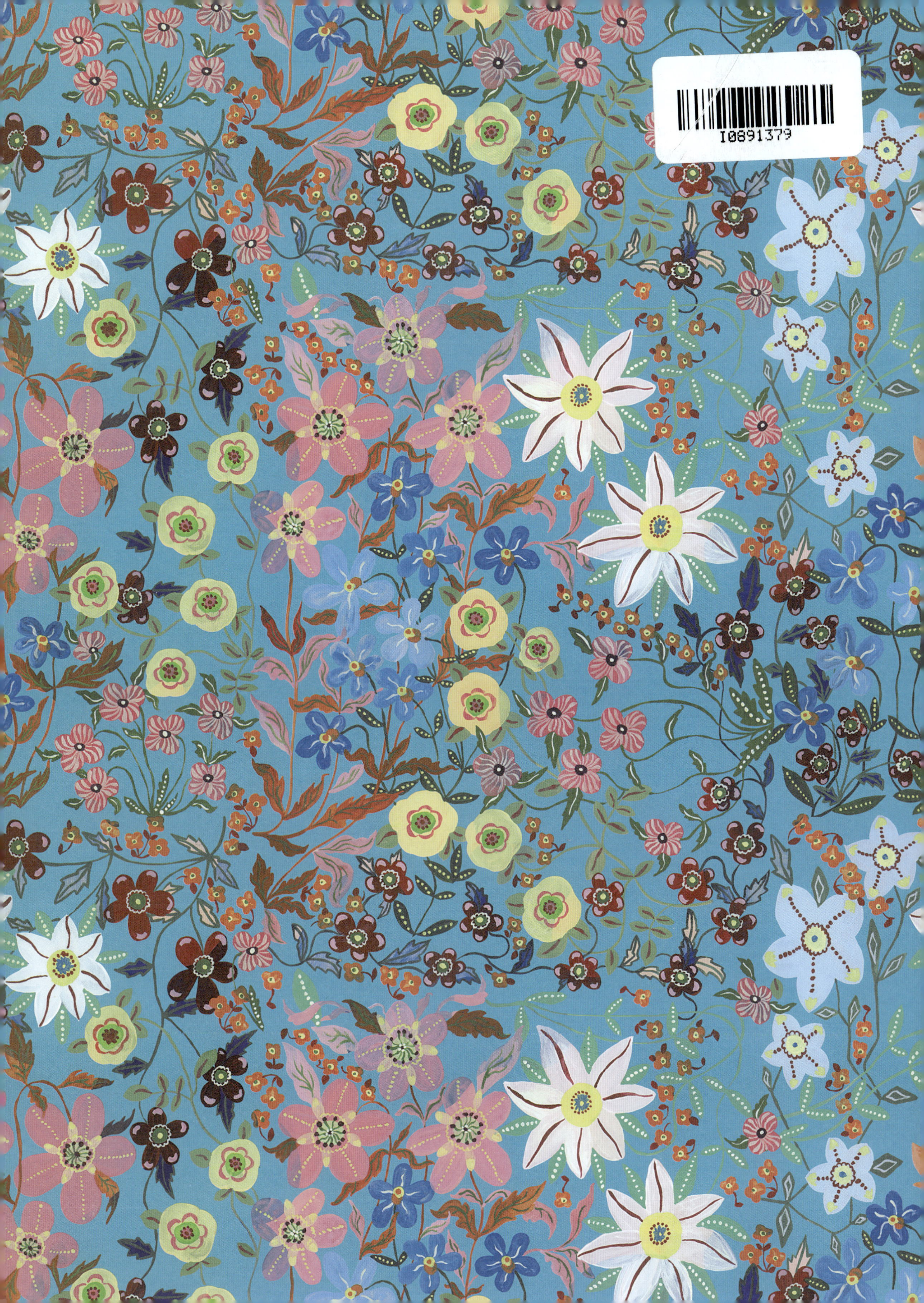

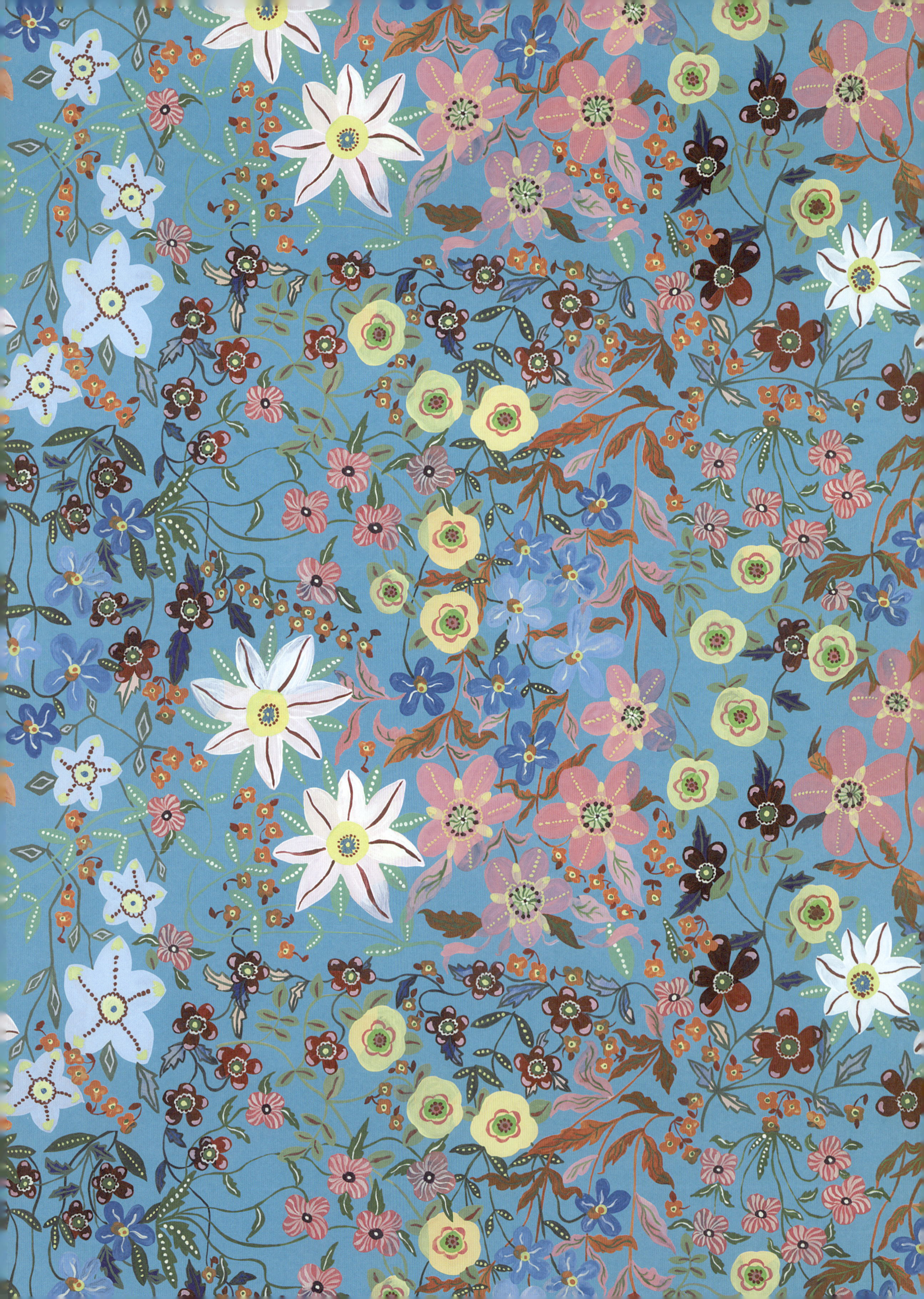

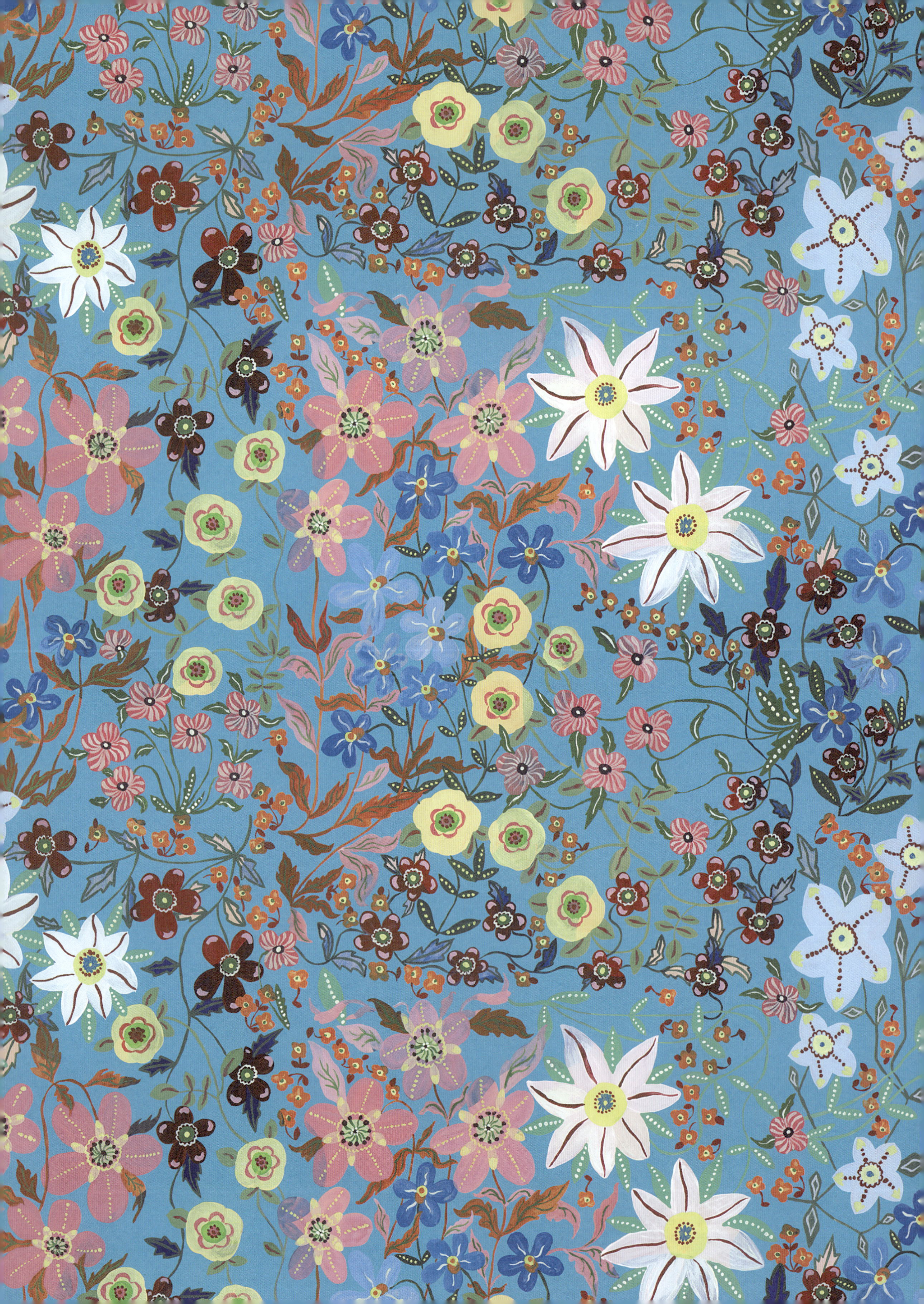

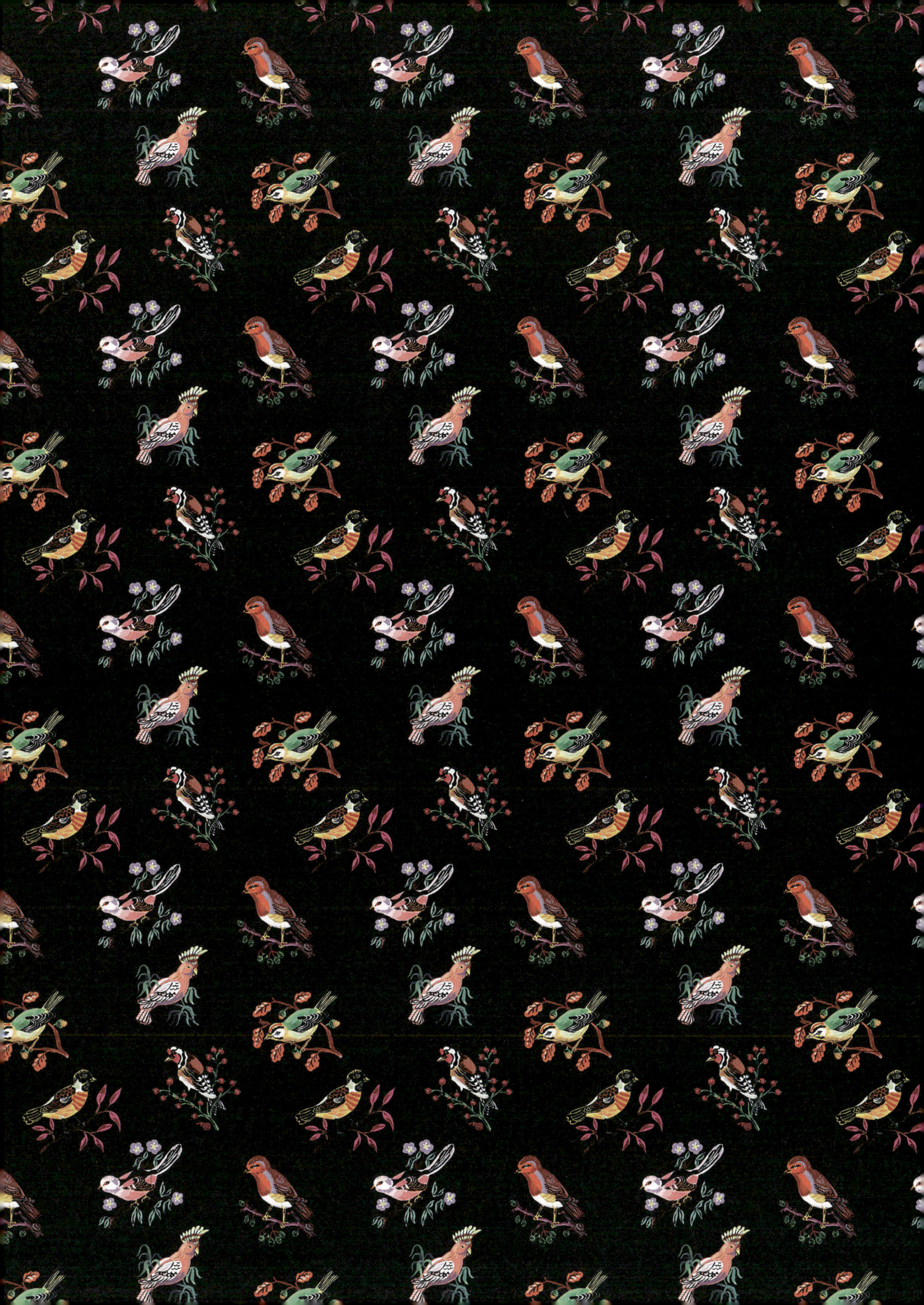

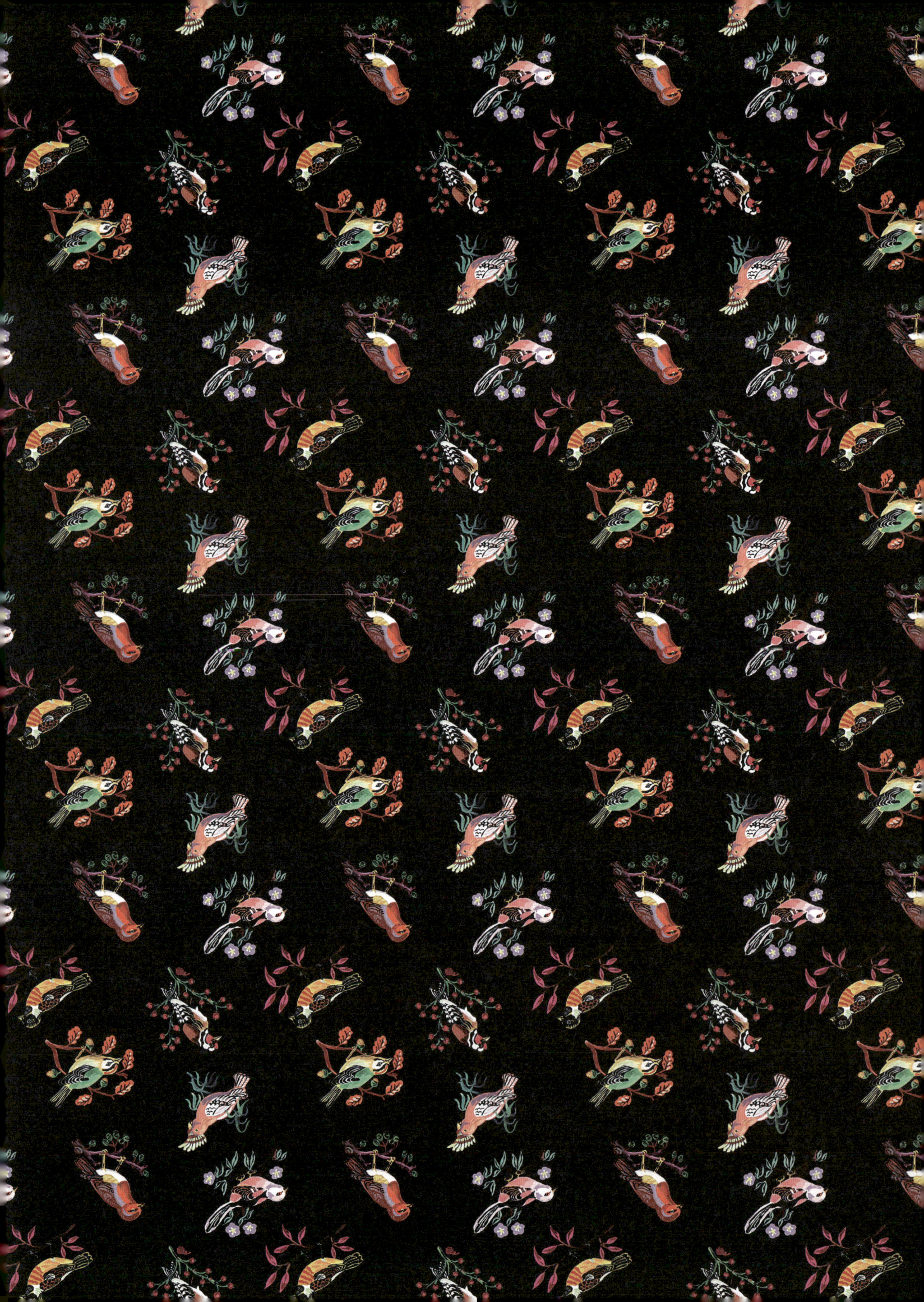

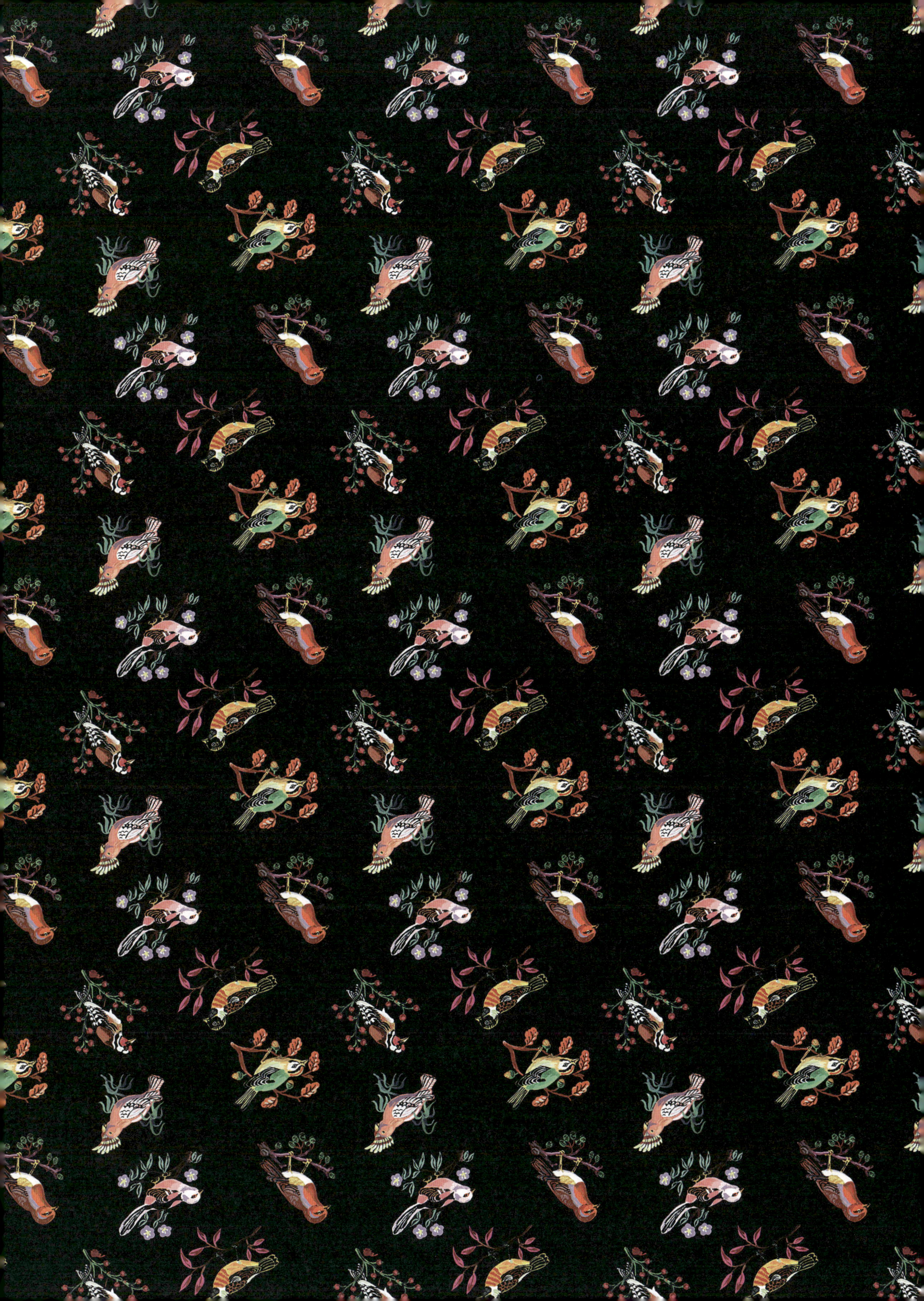

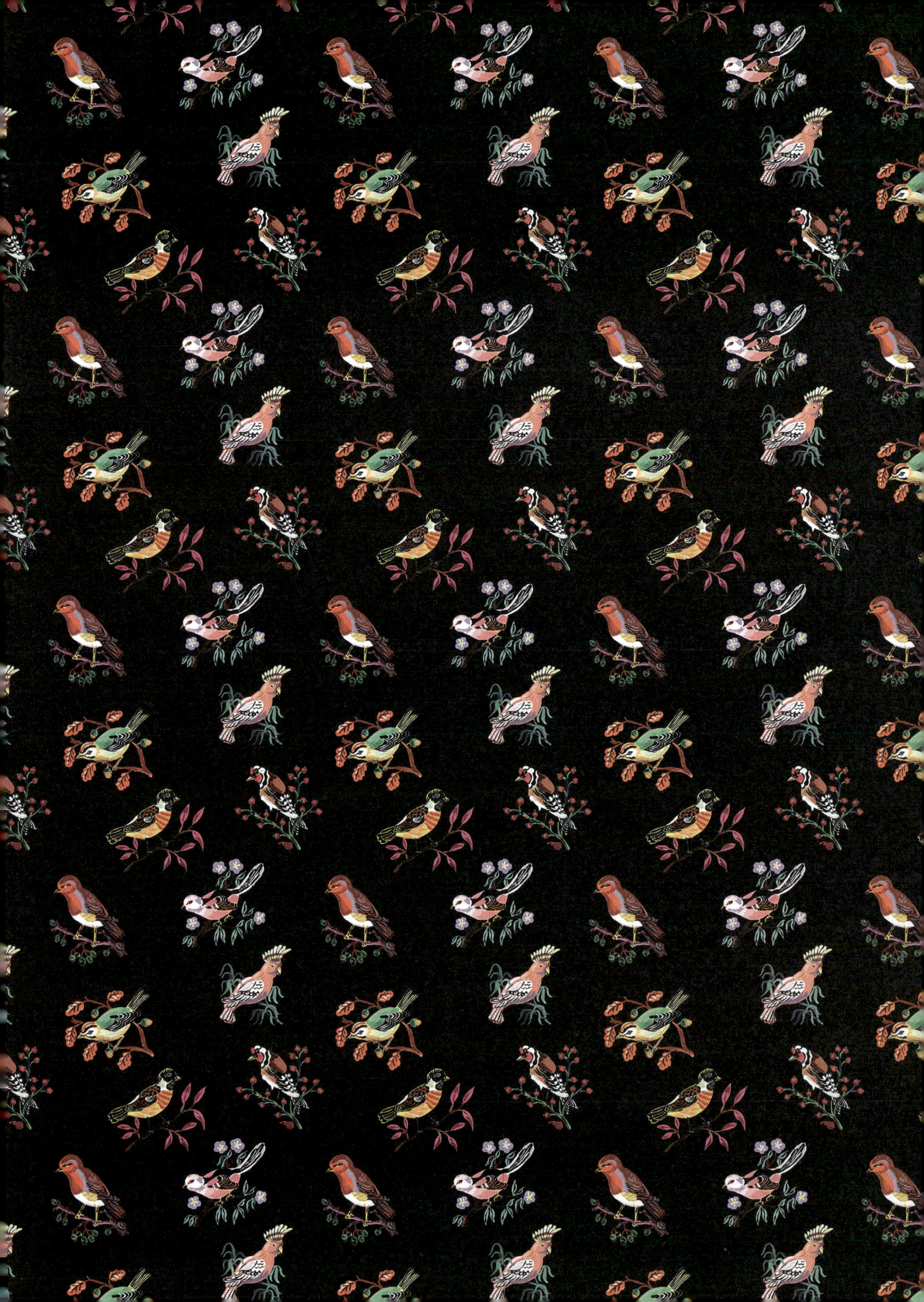

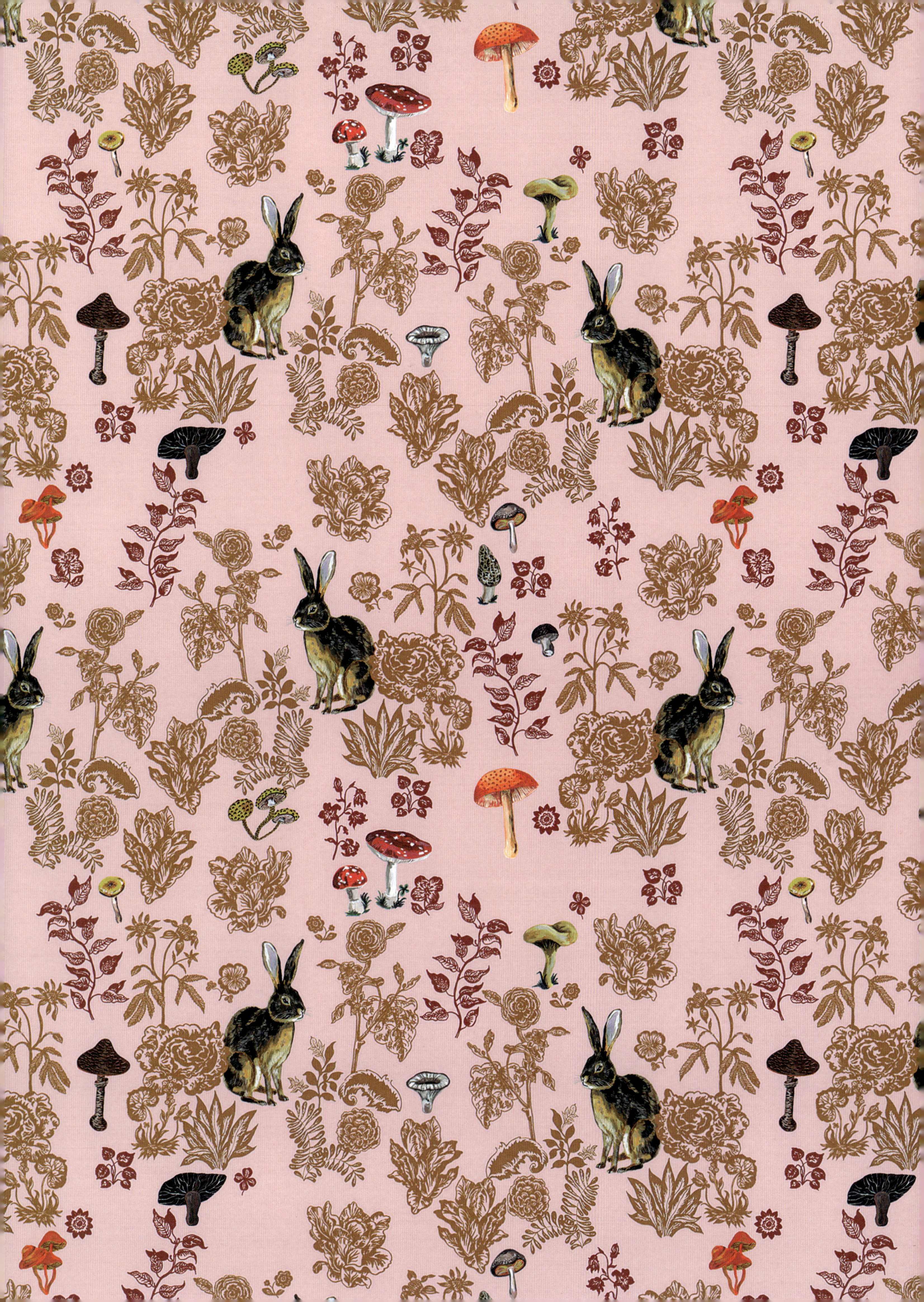

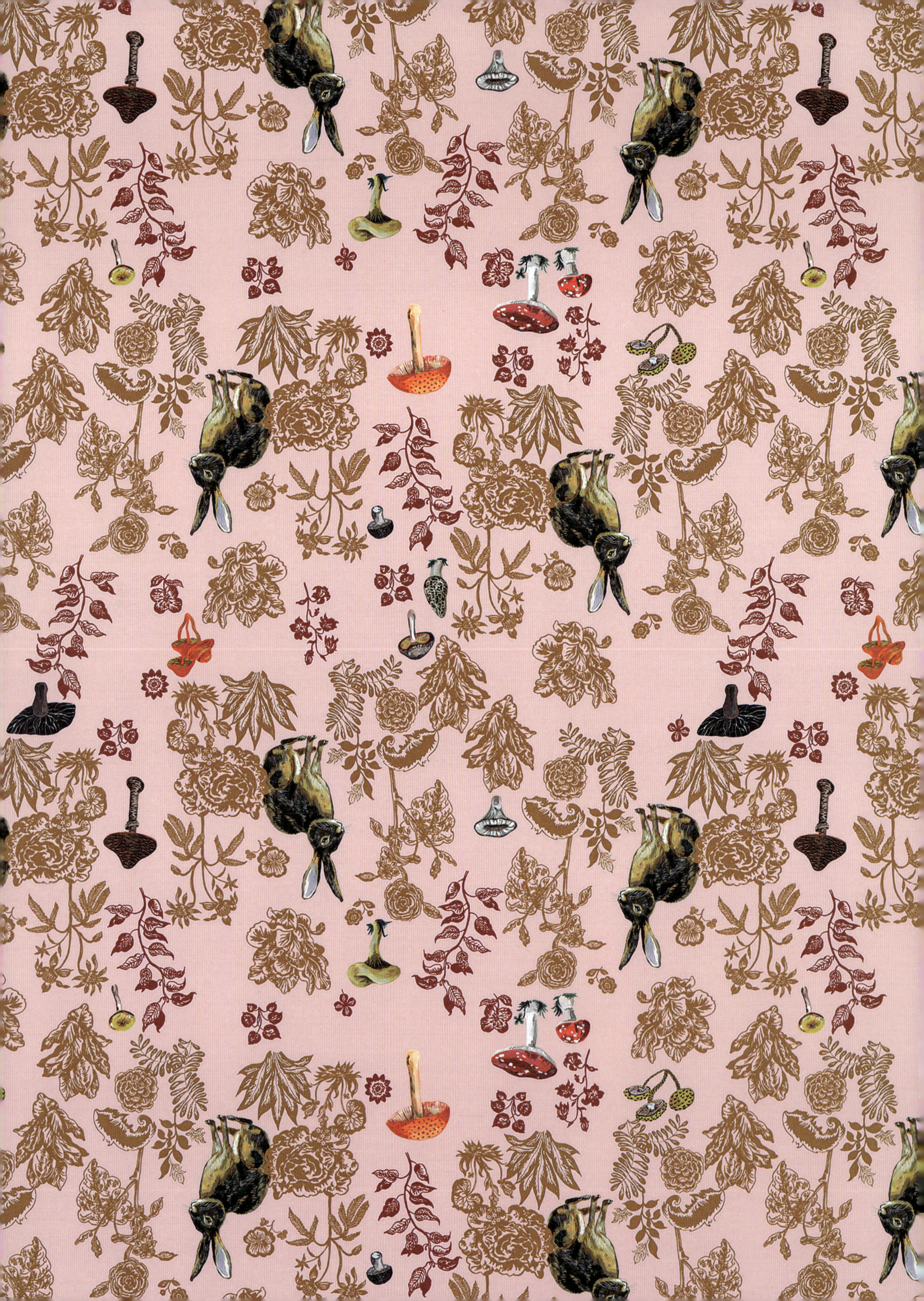

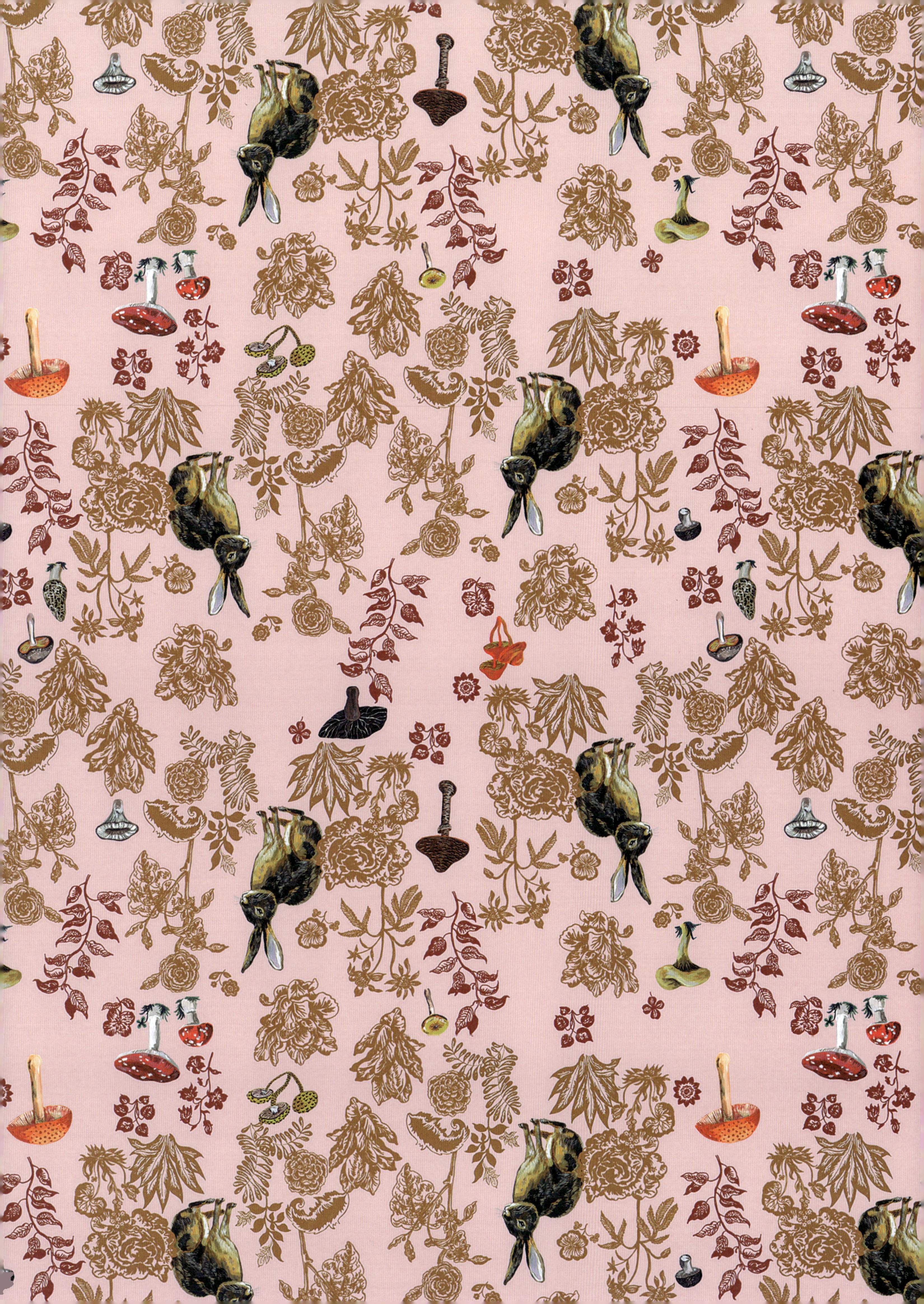

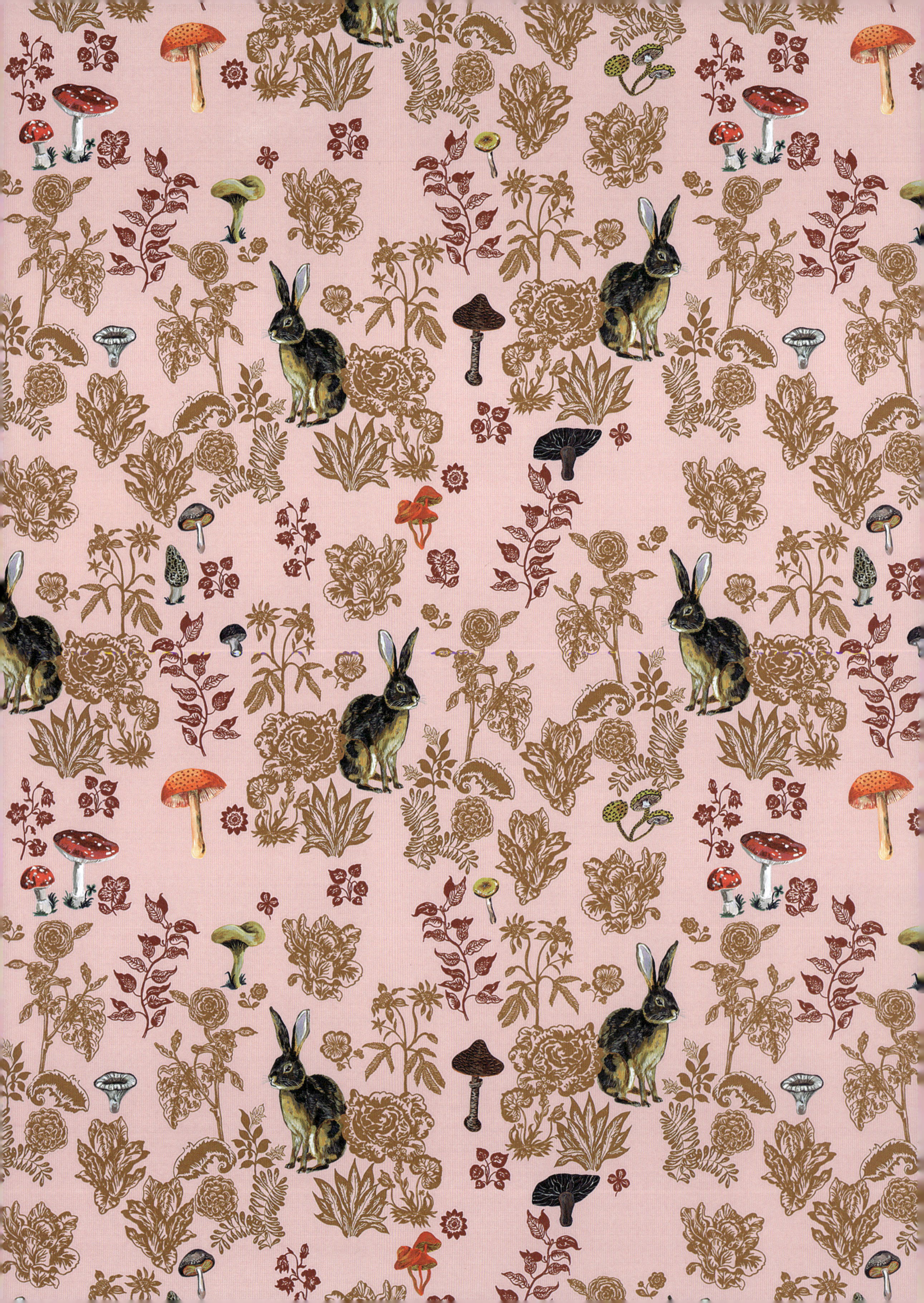

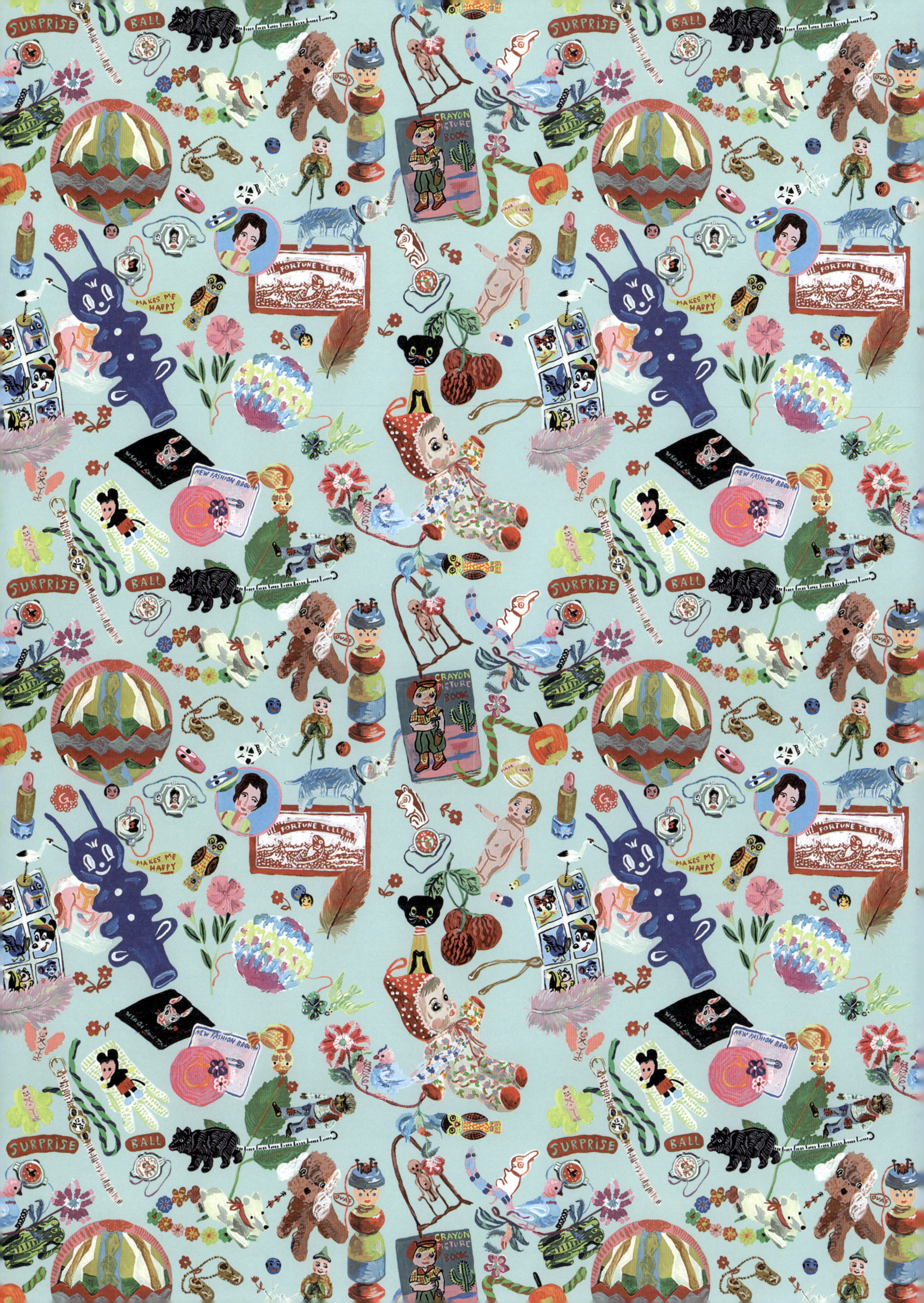
SURPRISE
BALL
CRAYON PICTURE BOOK
FORTUNE TELLER
MAKES ME HAPPY

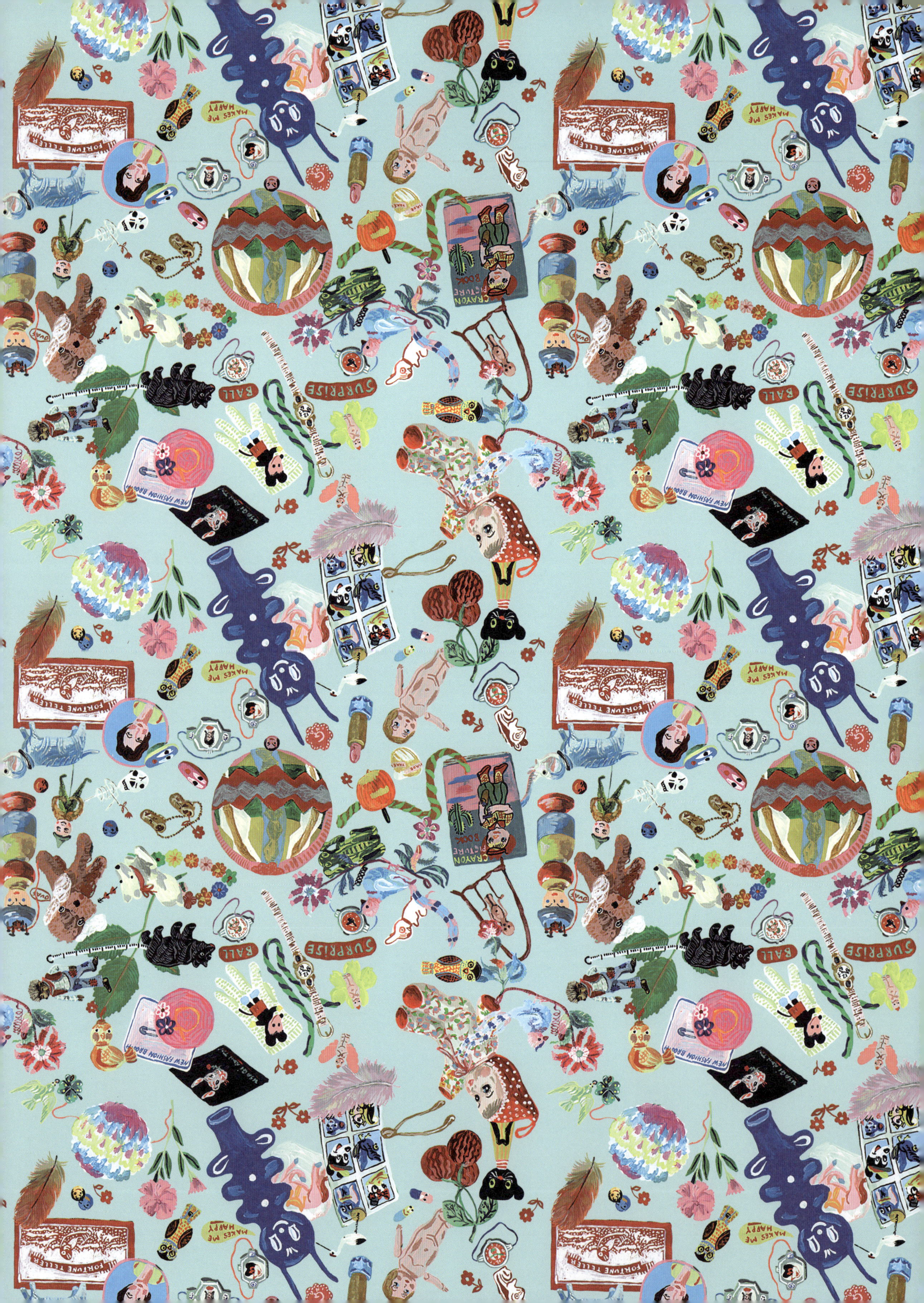

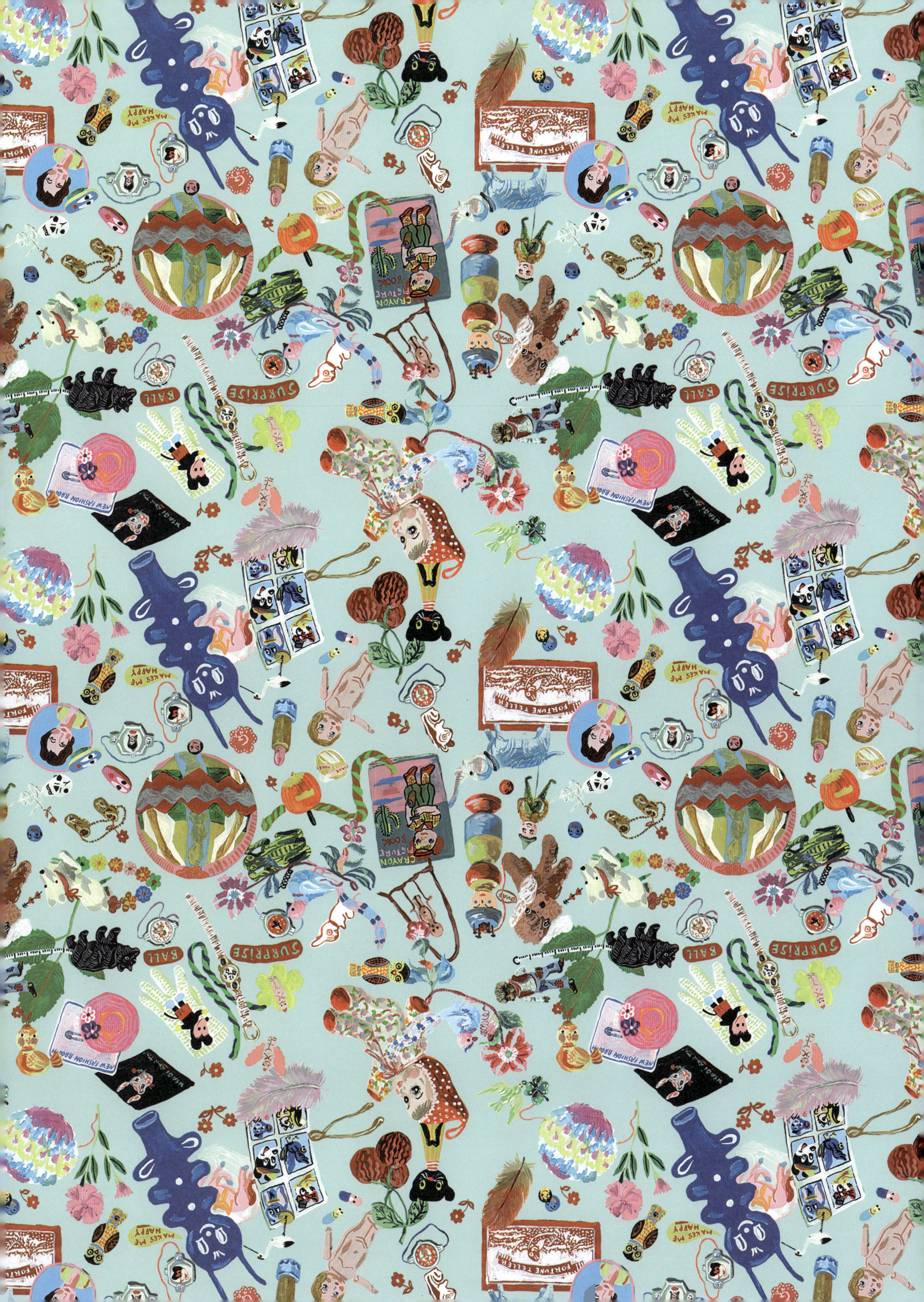
MAKES ME HAPPY
FORTUNE TELLER
SURPRISE
BALL
CRAYON PICTURE BOOK
NEW FASHION BROOCH

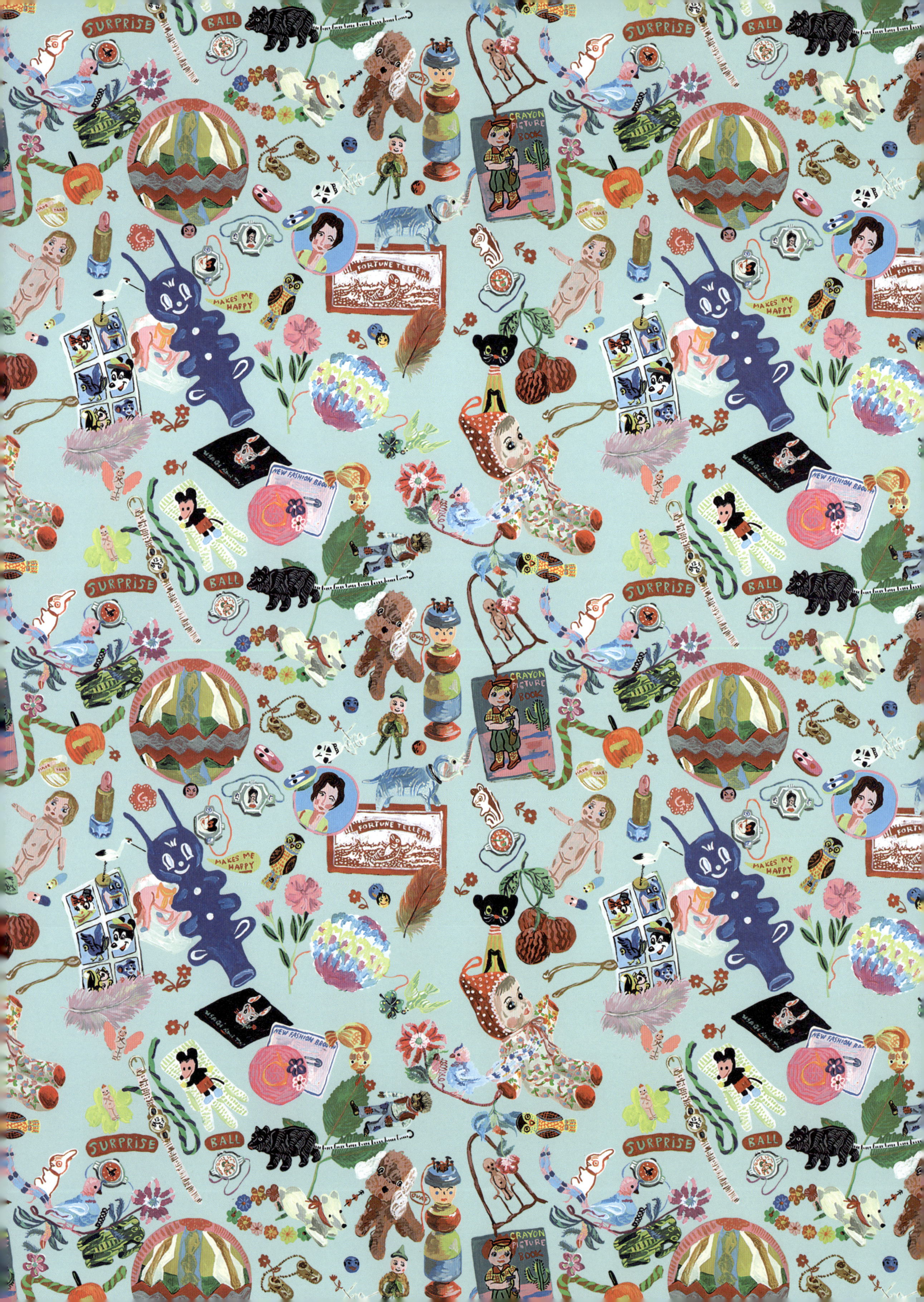
SURPRISE
BALL
CRAYON PICTURE BOOK
FORTUNE TELLER
MAKES ME HAPPY

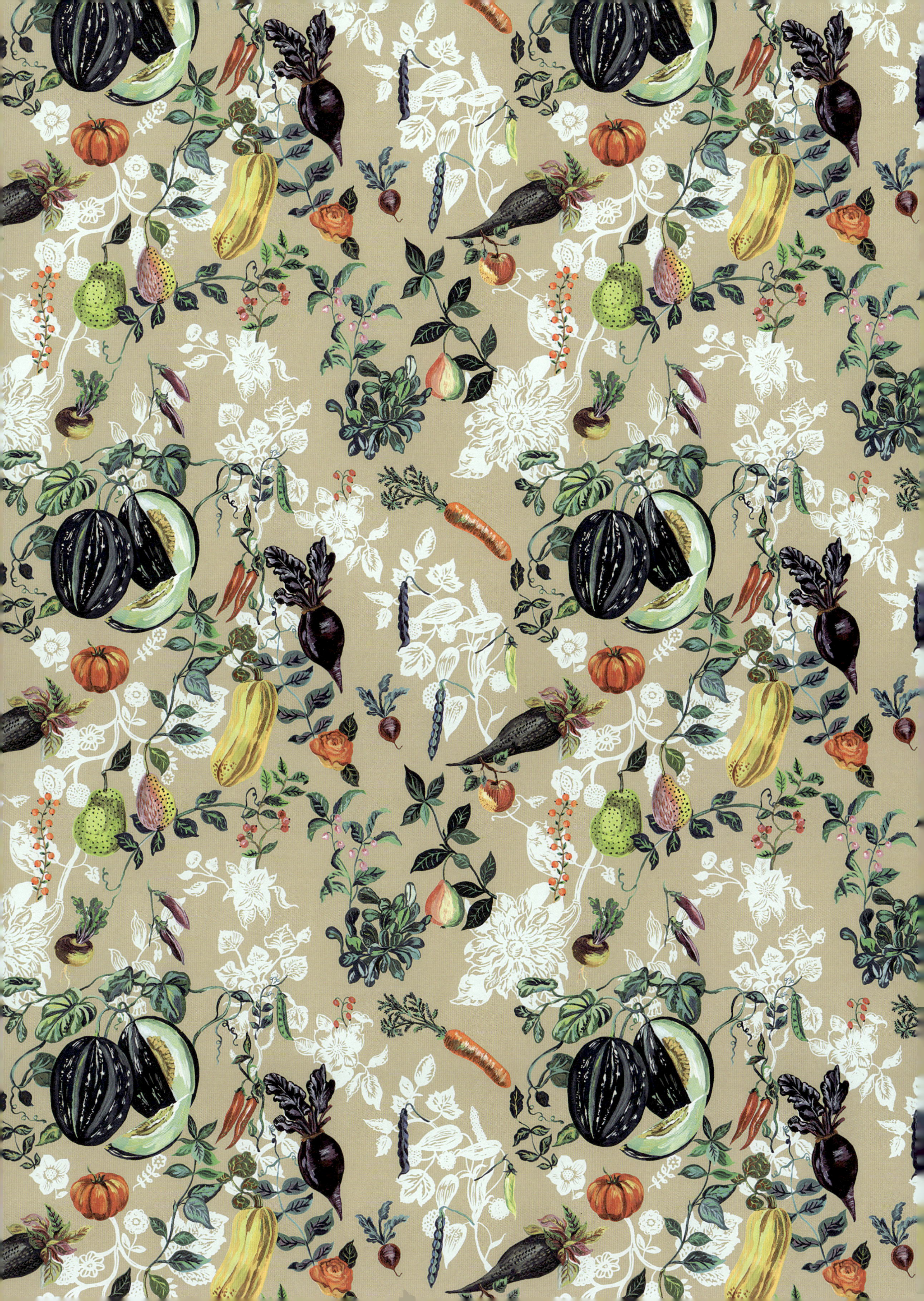

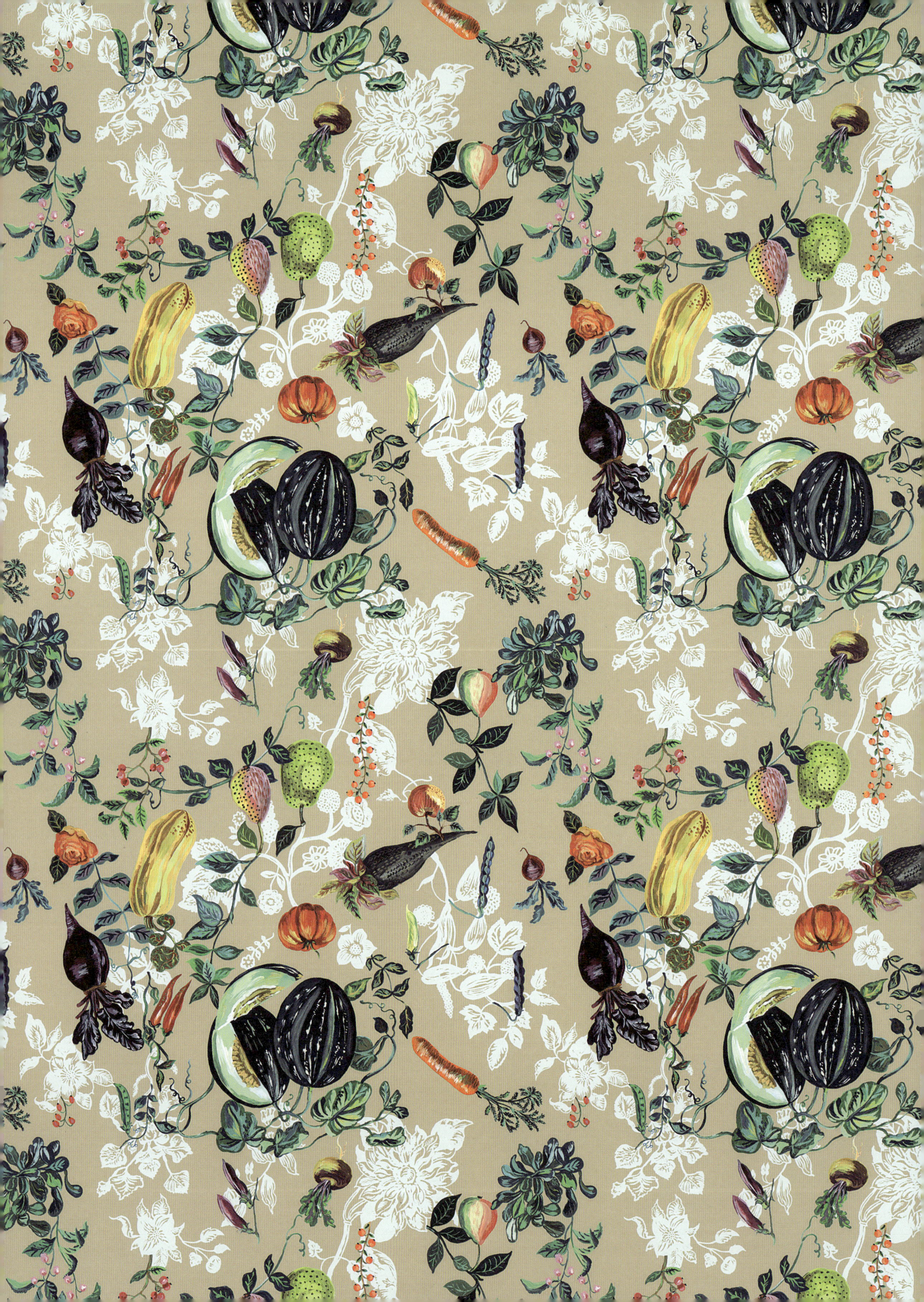

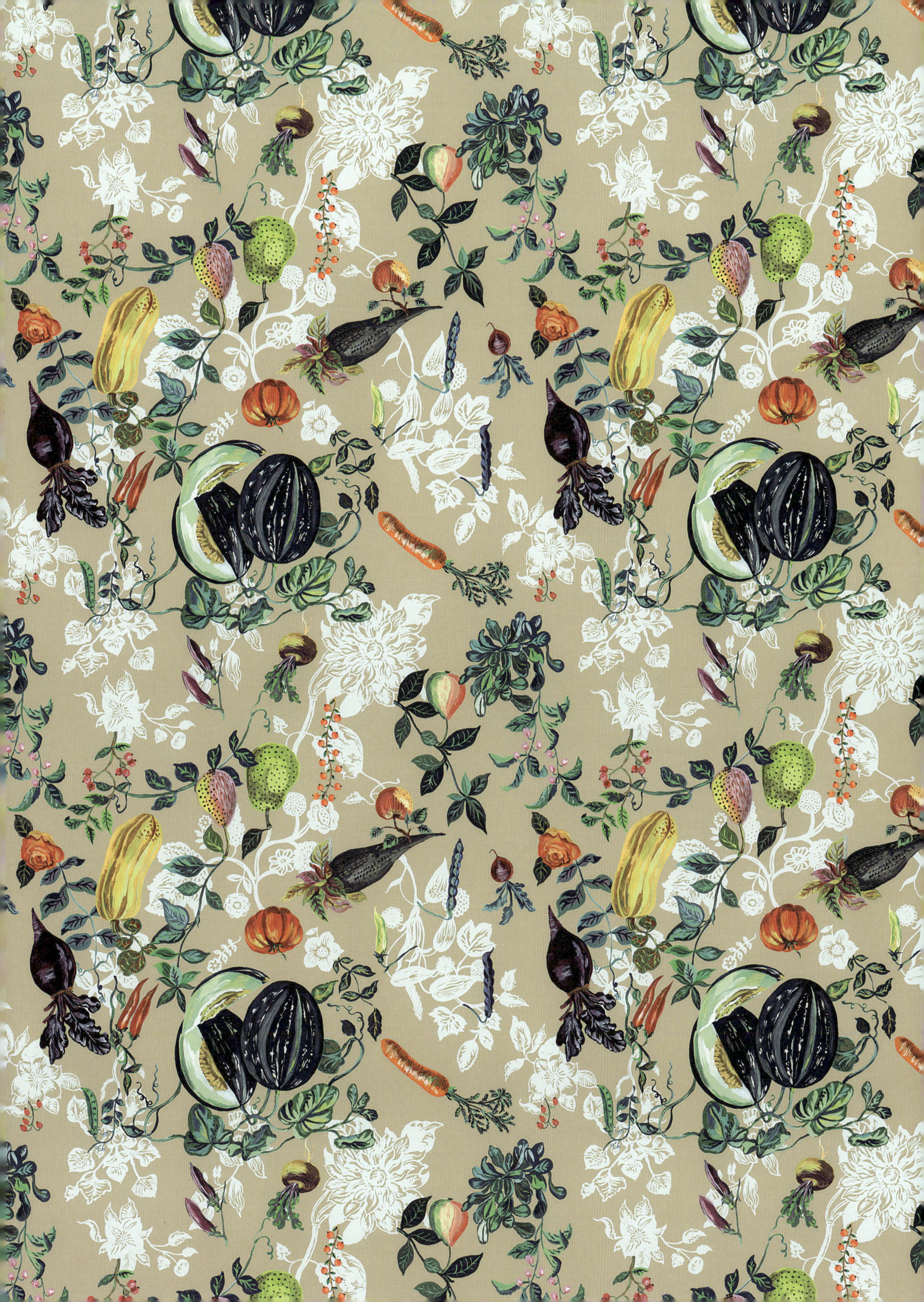

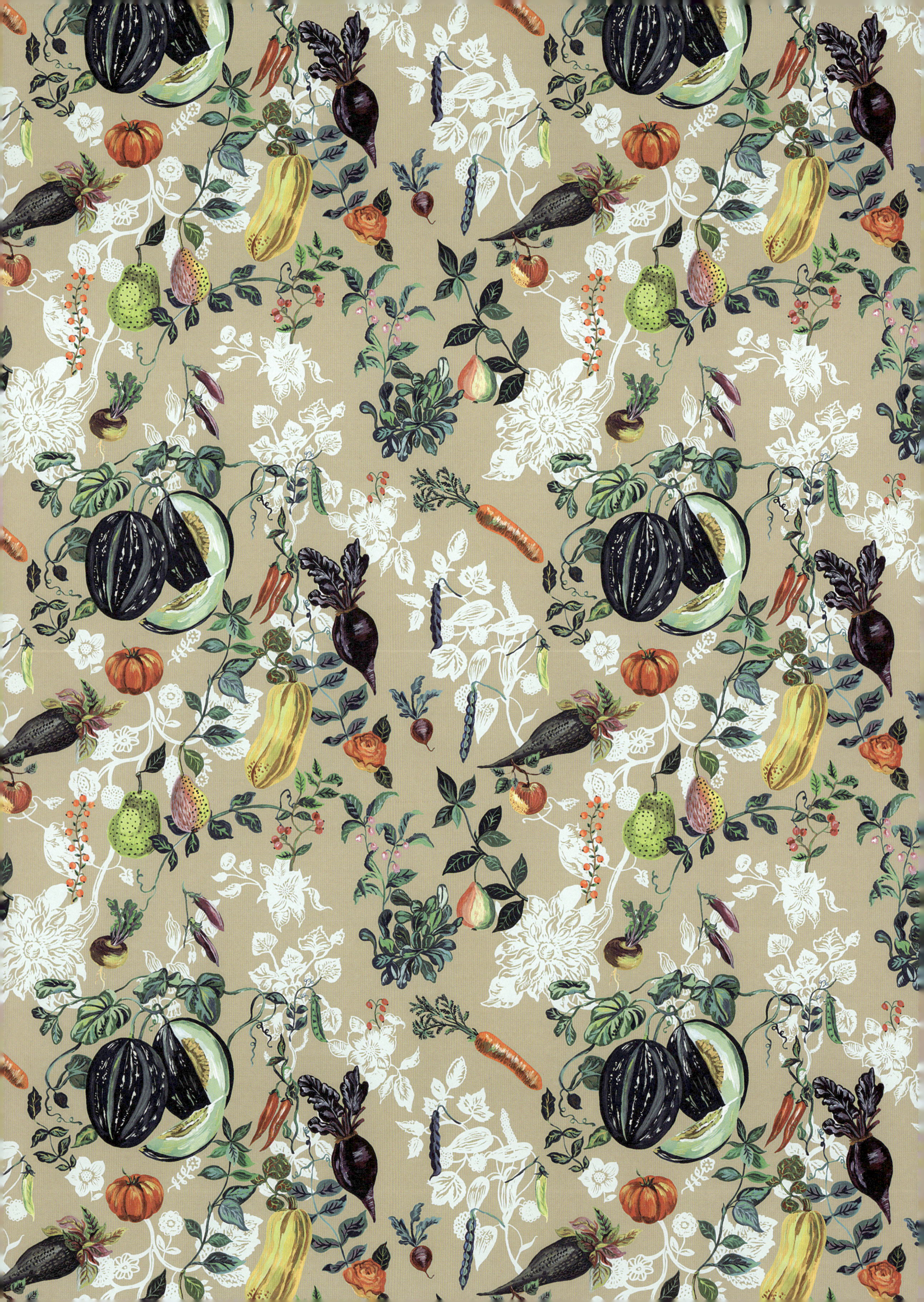

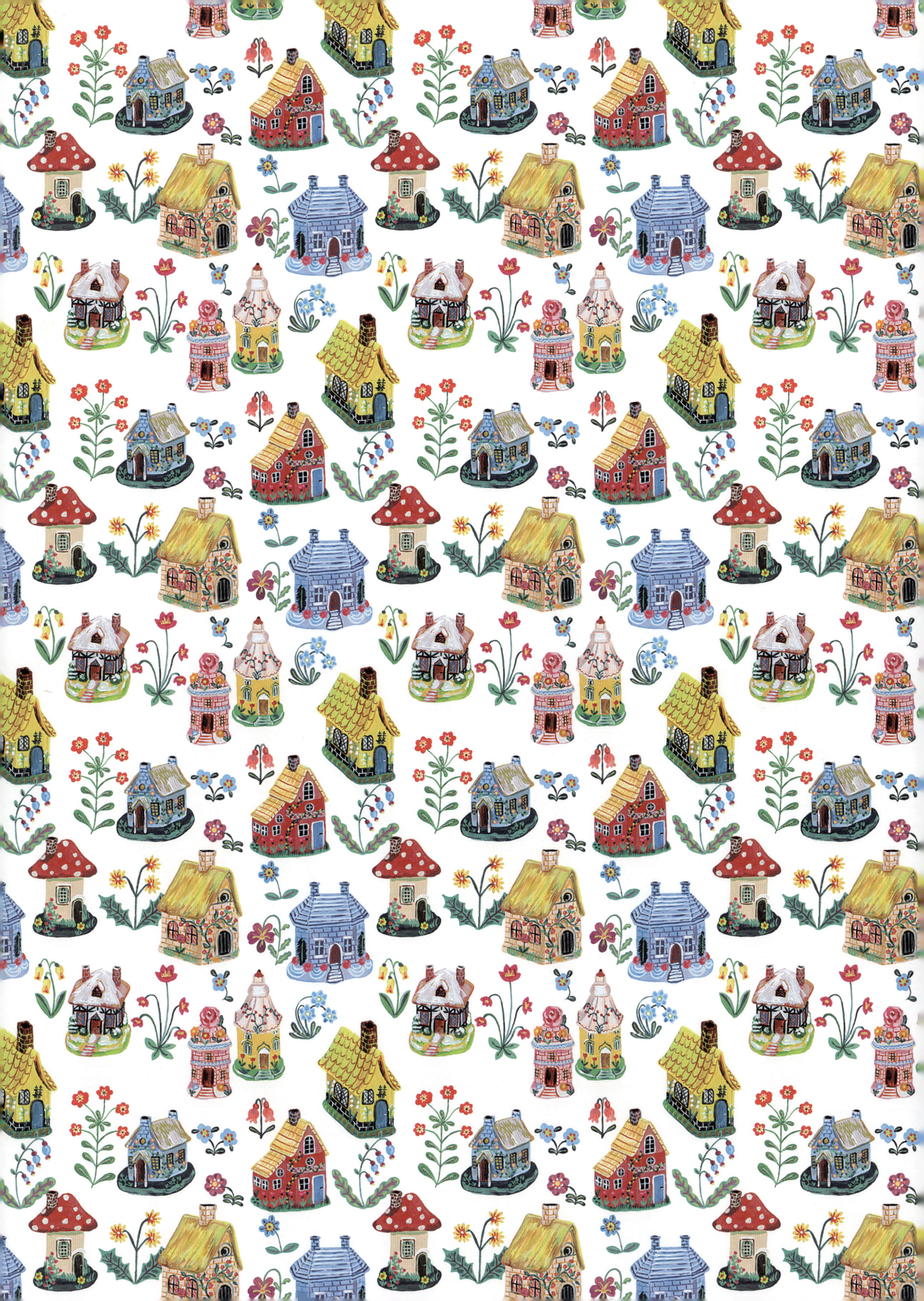

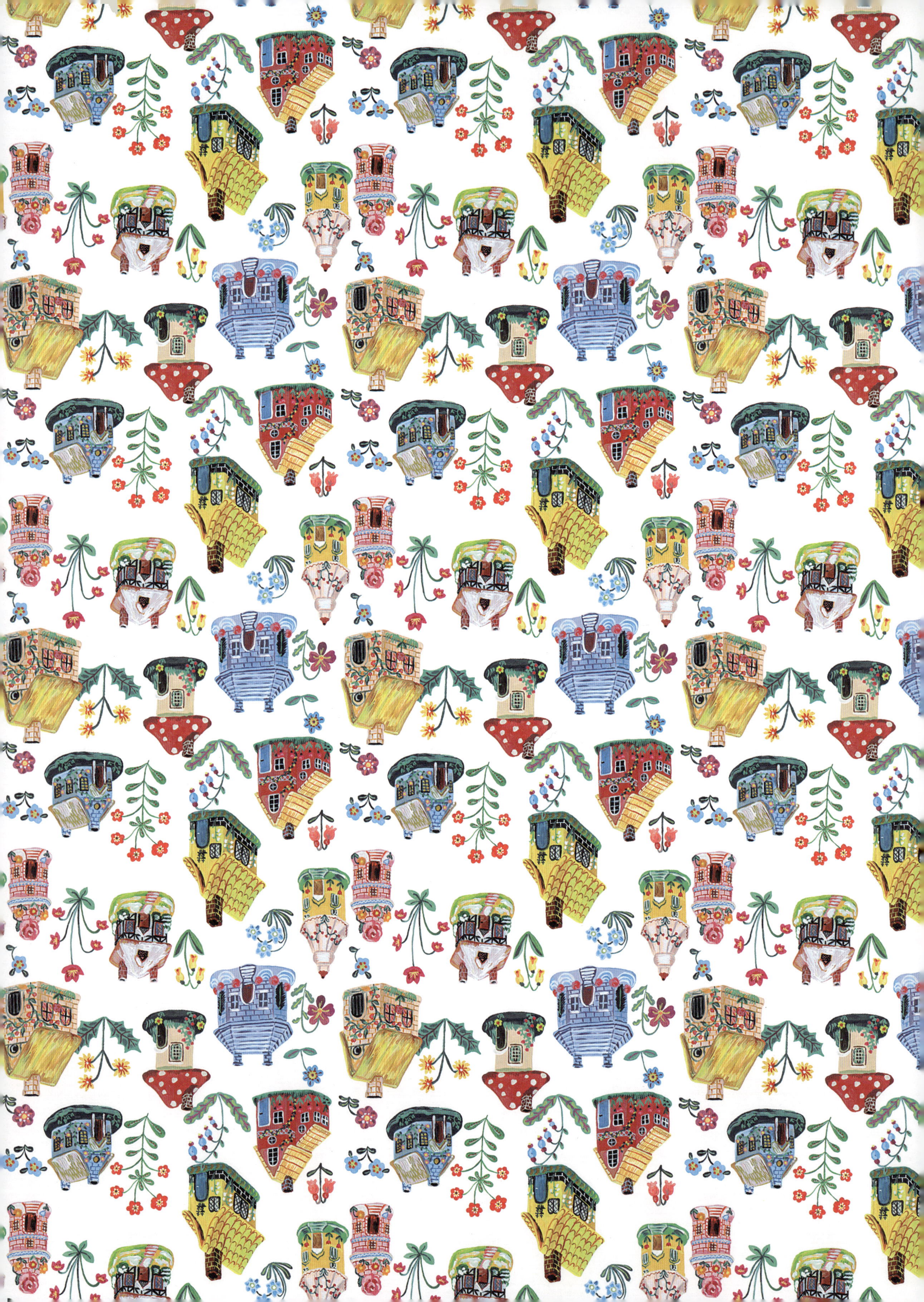

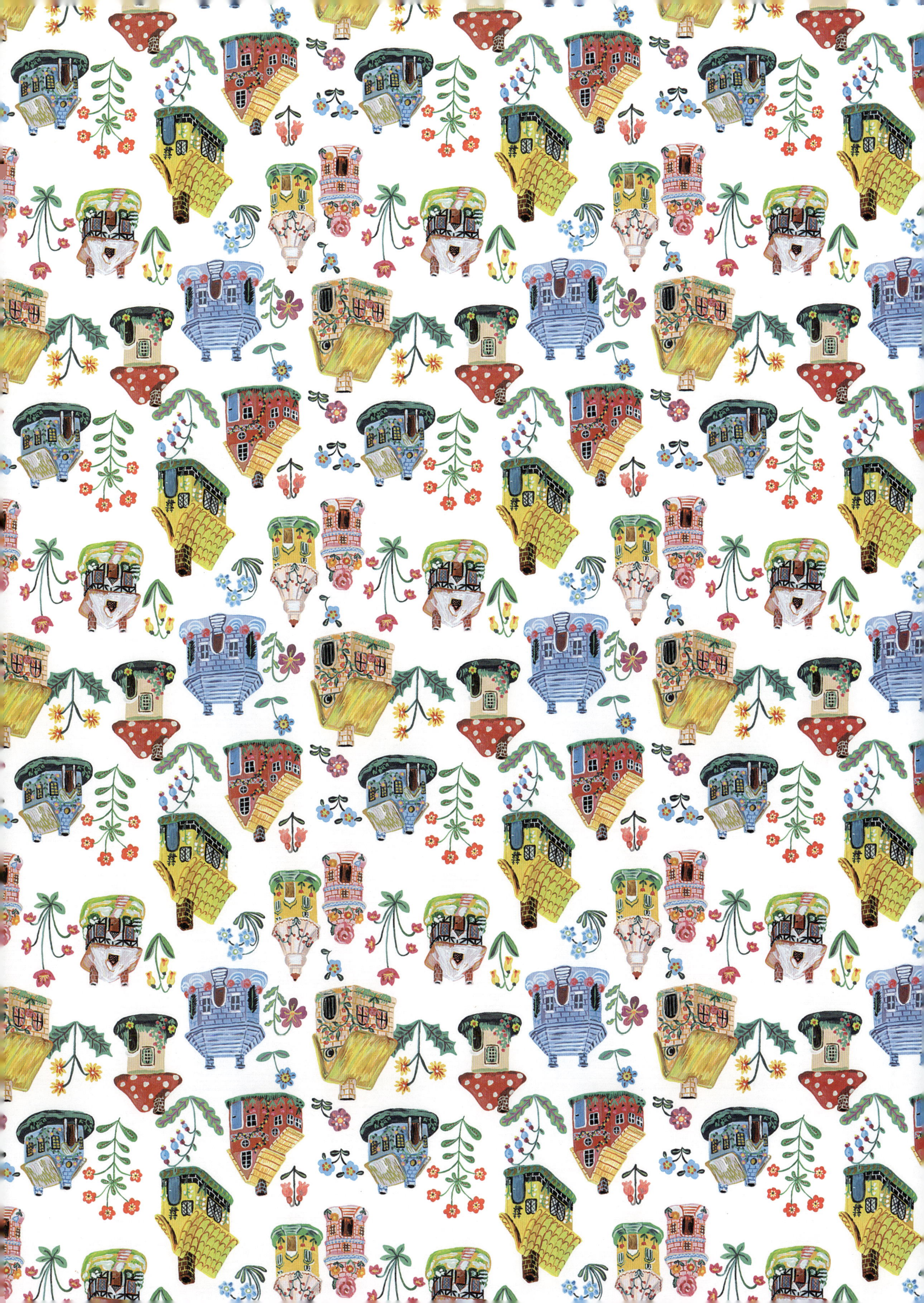

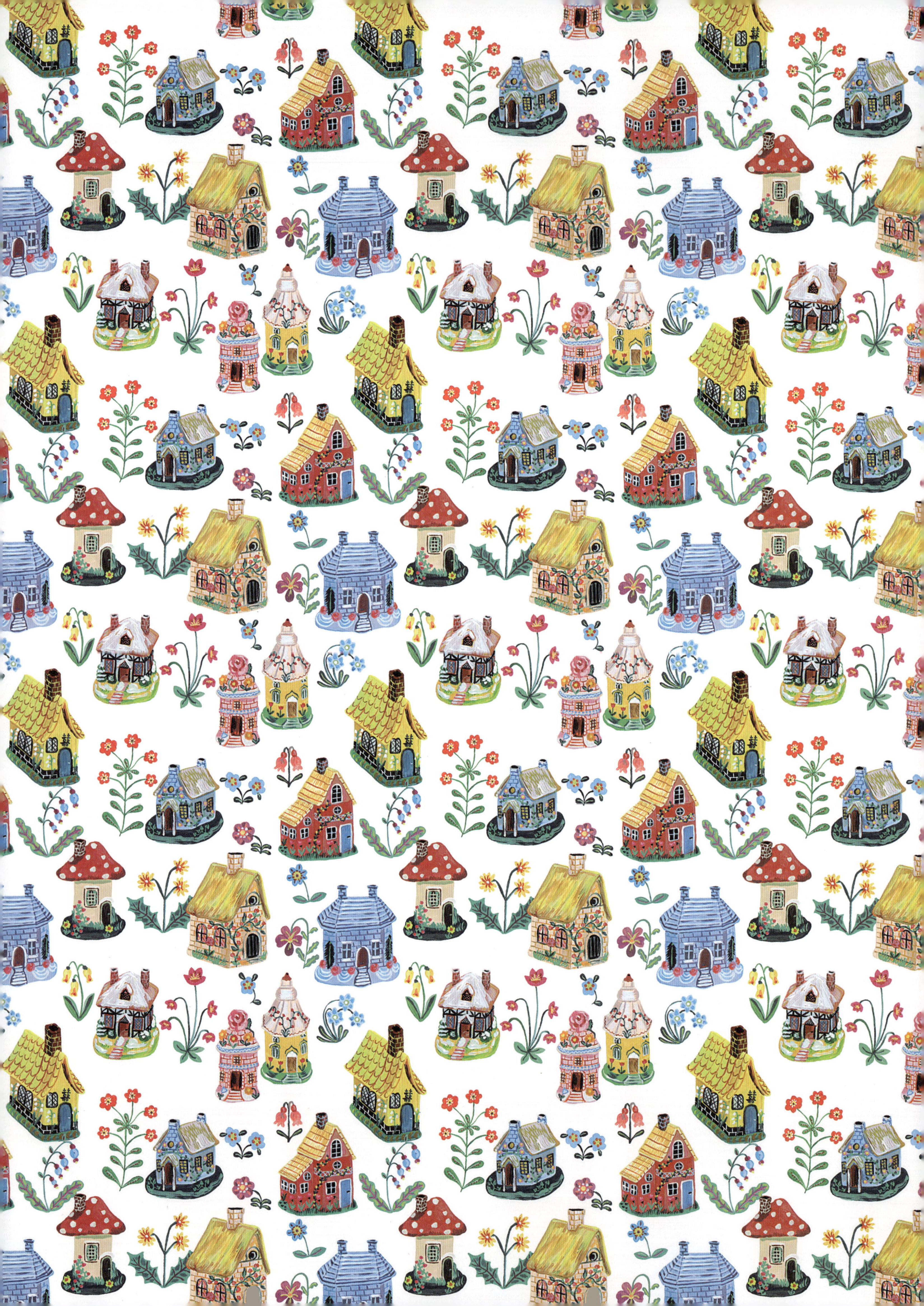

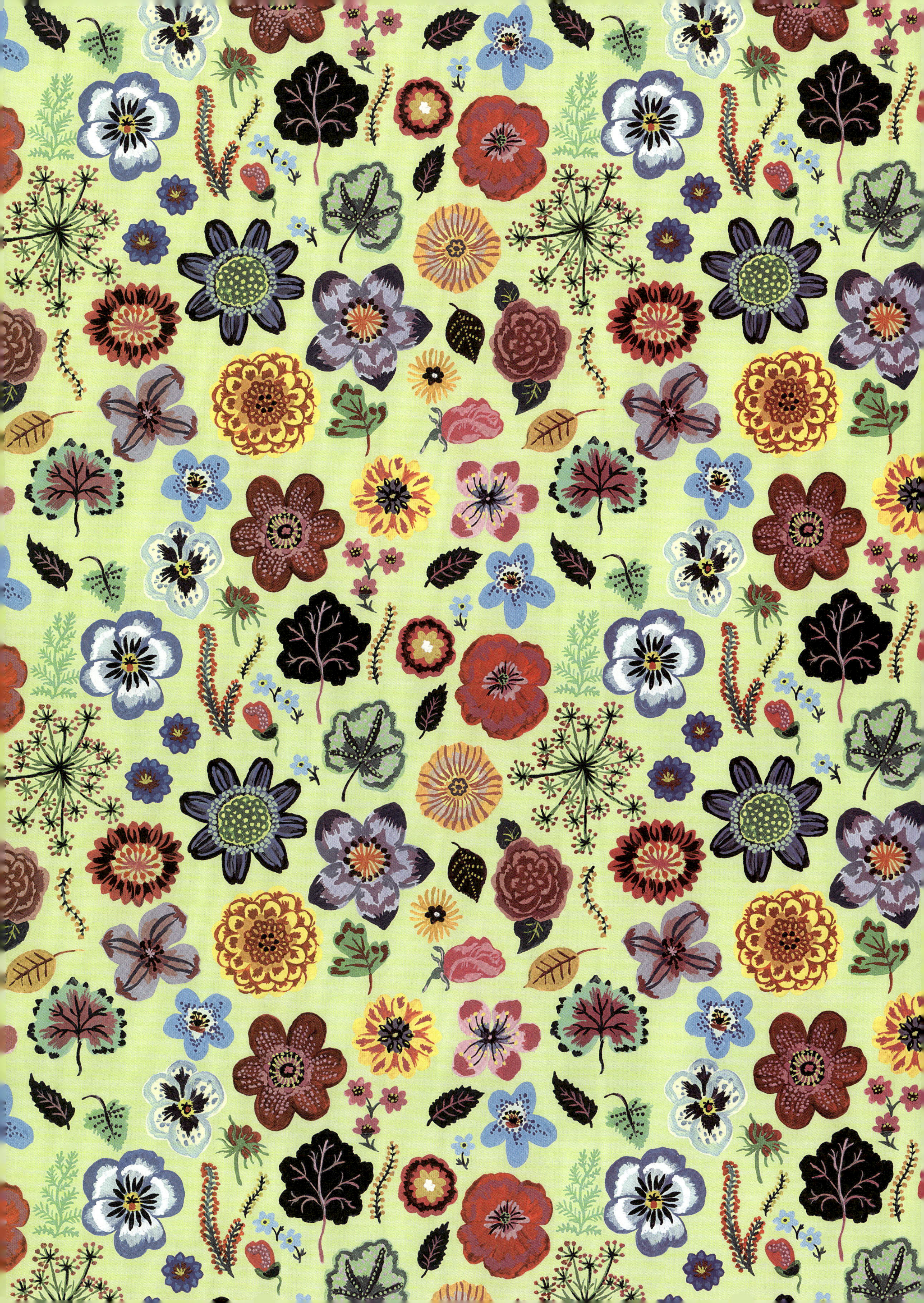

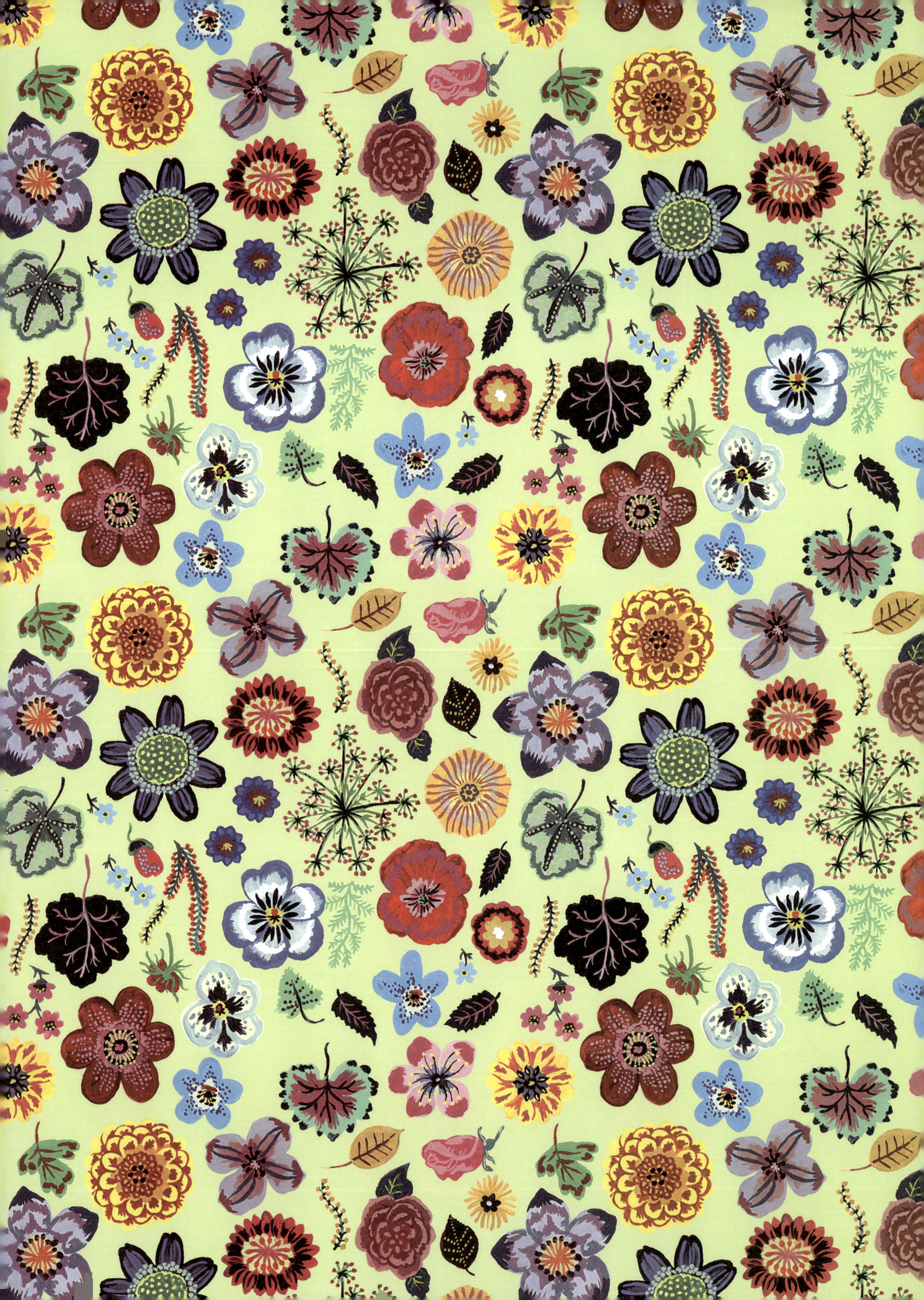

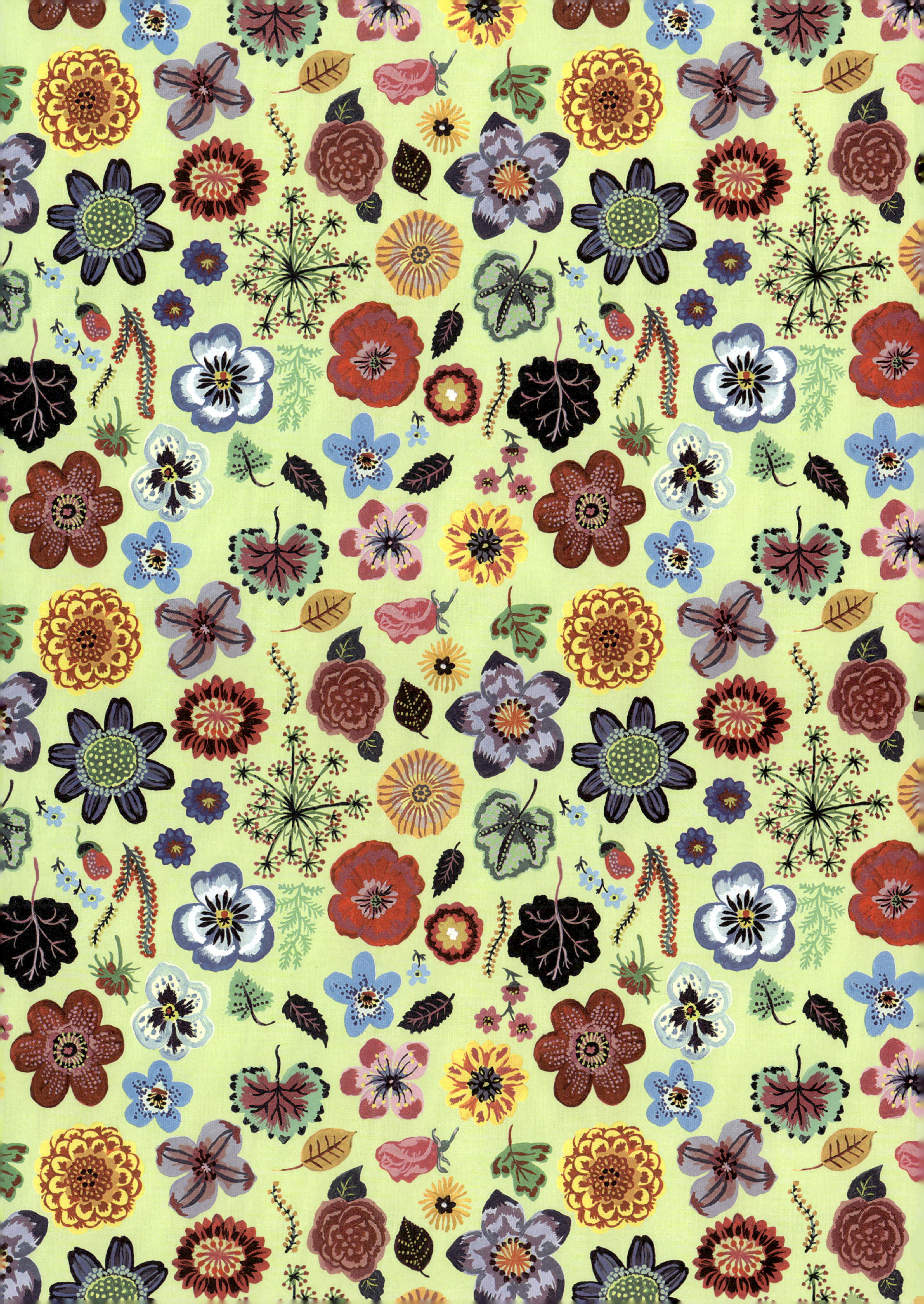

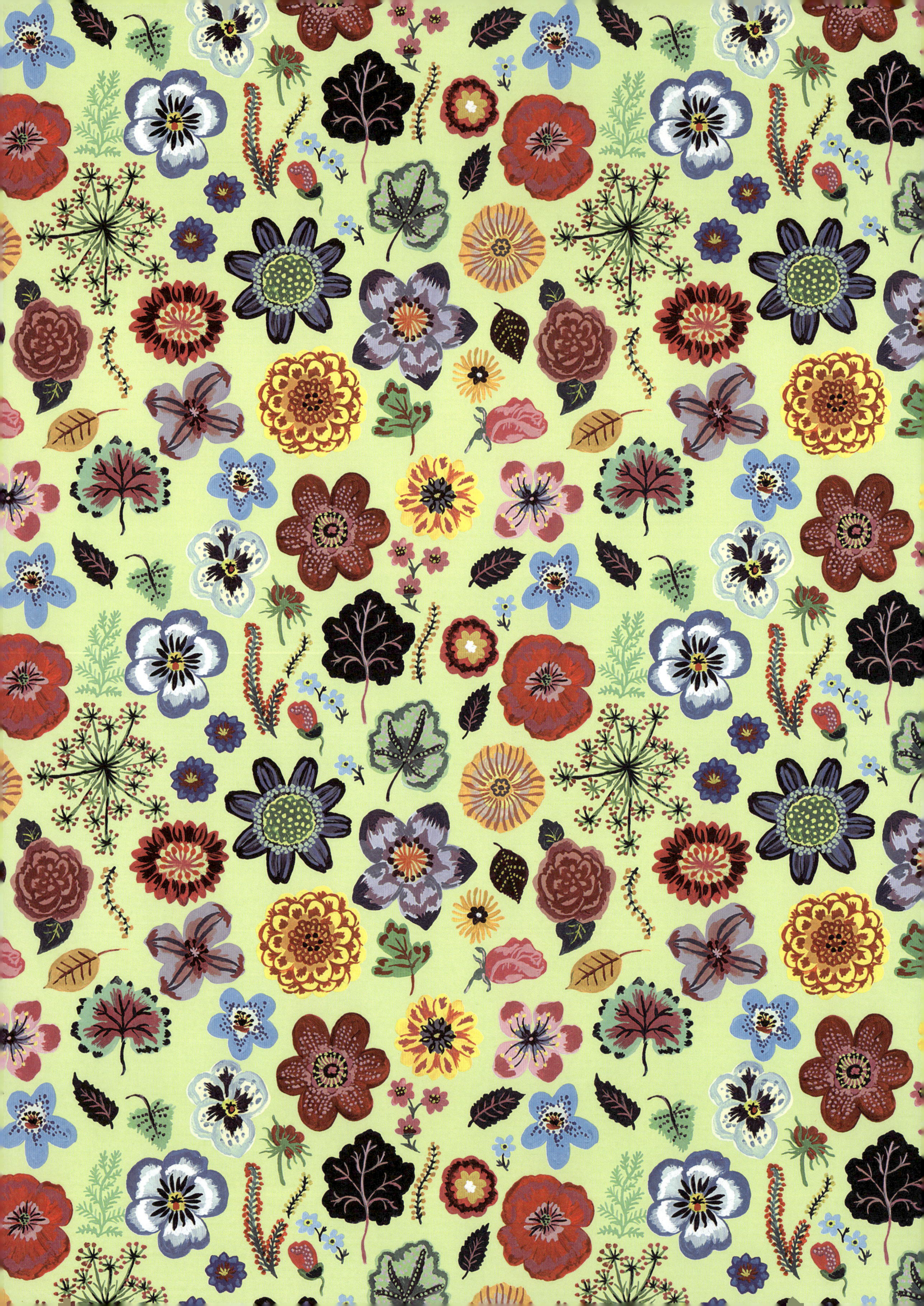

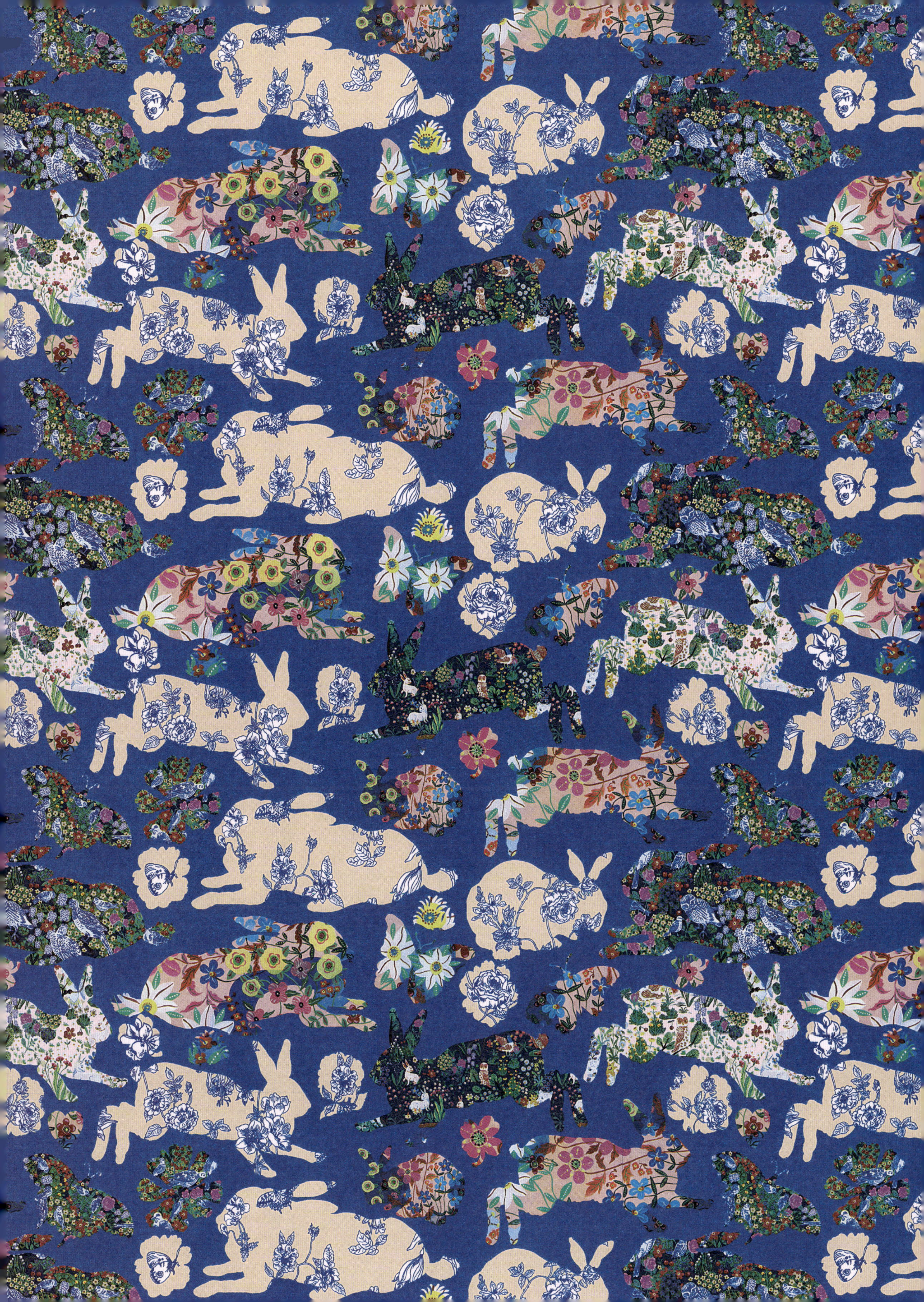

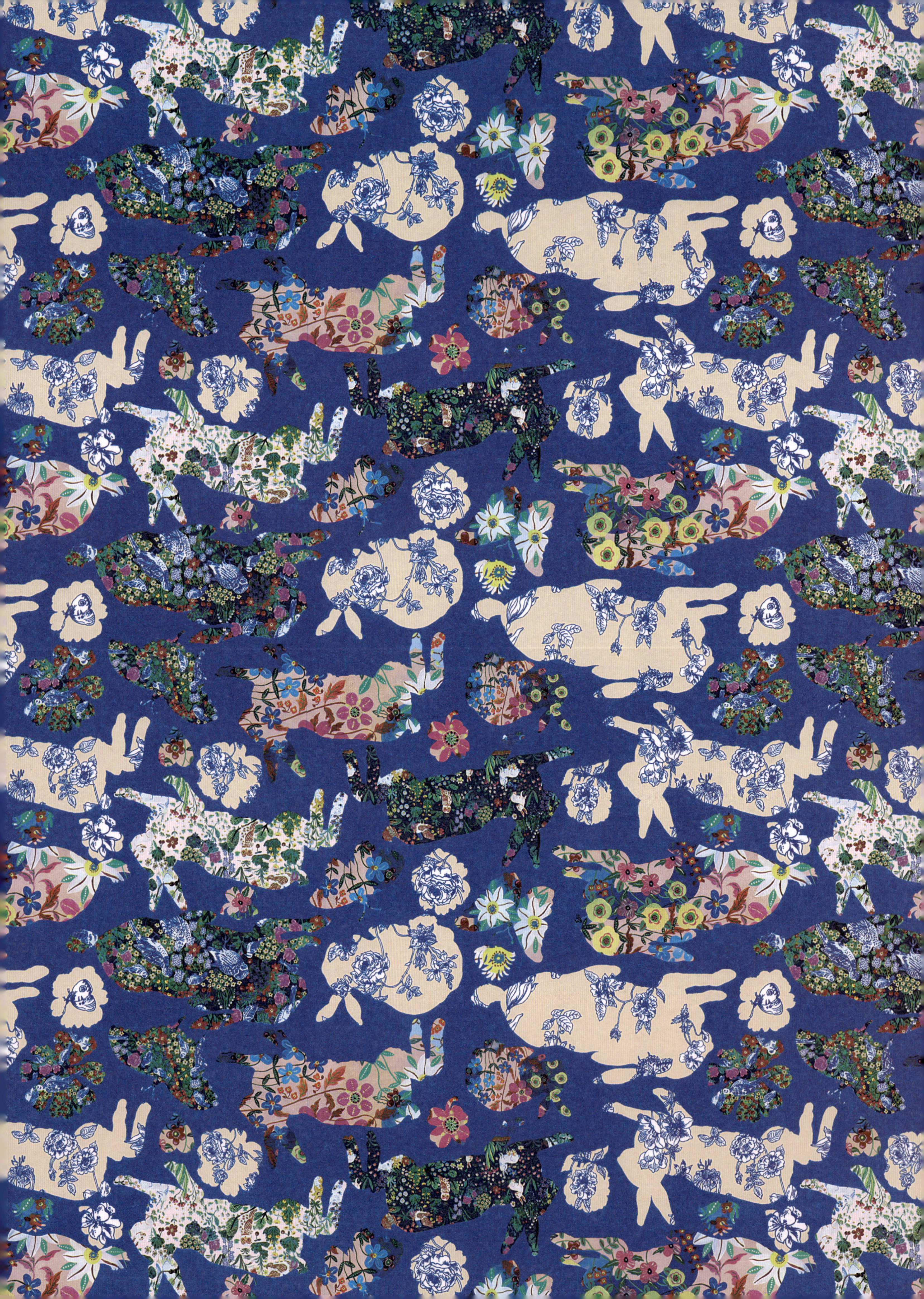

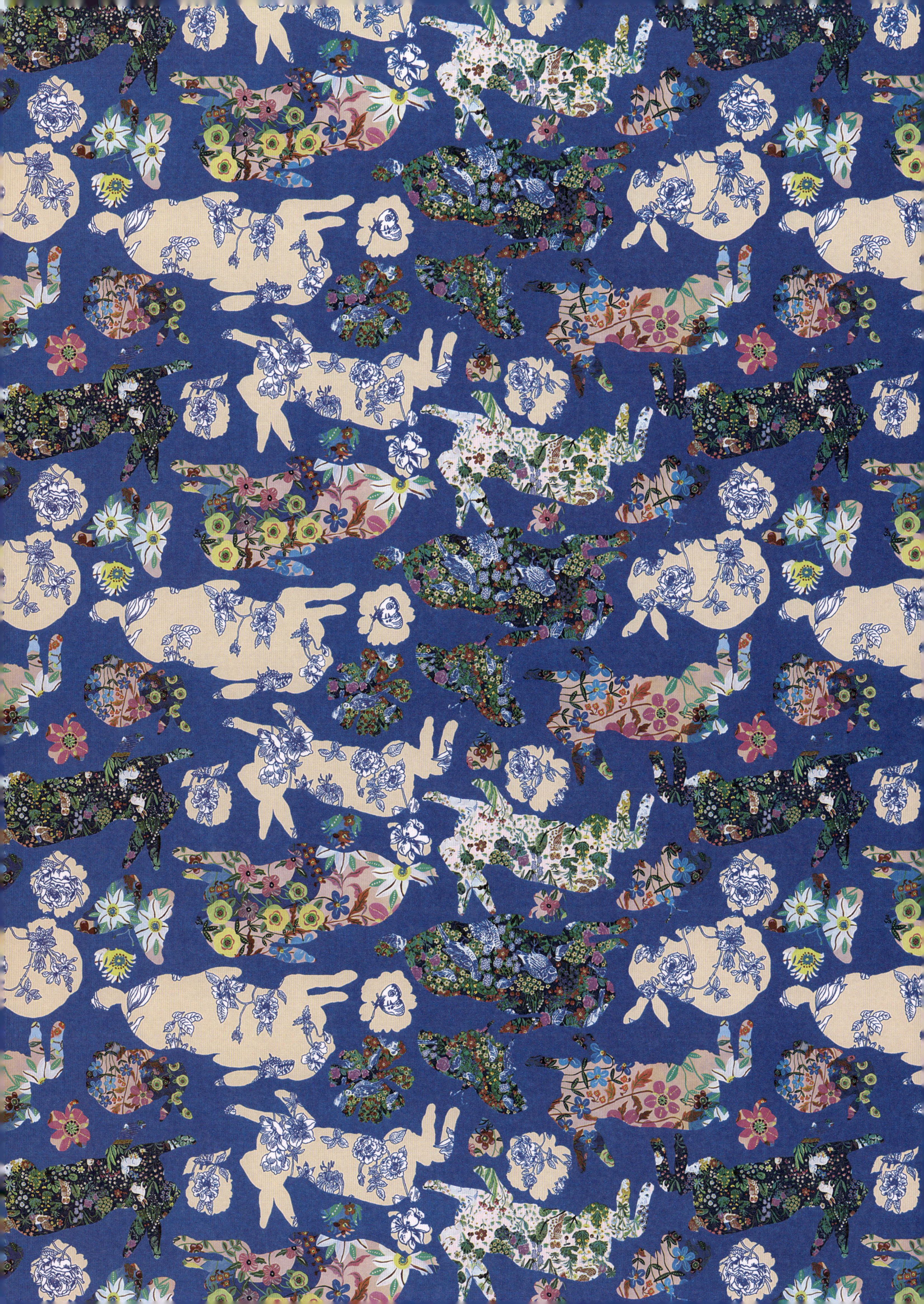

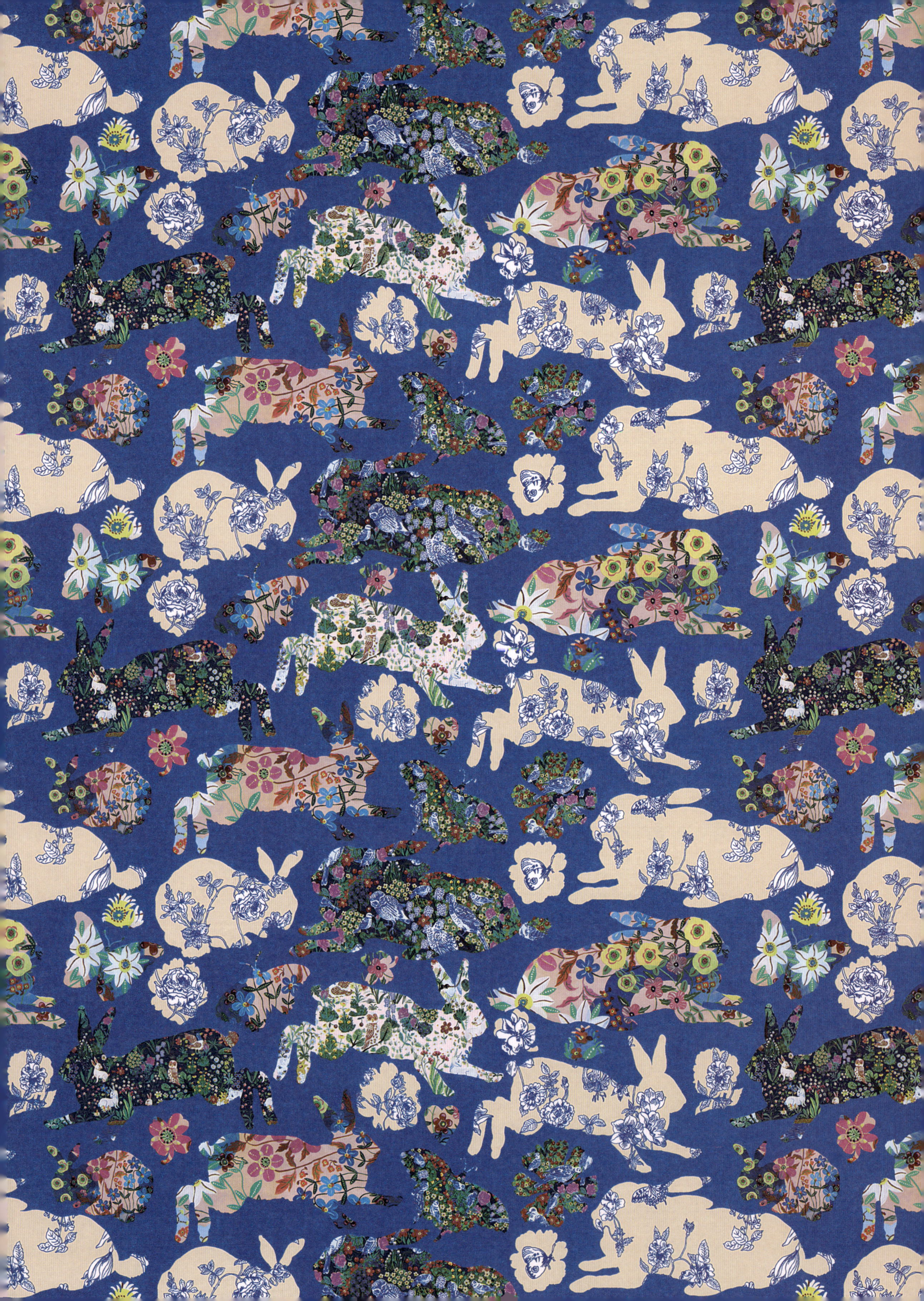

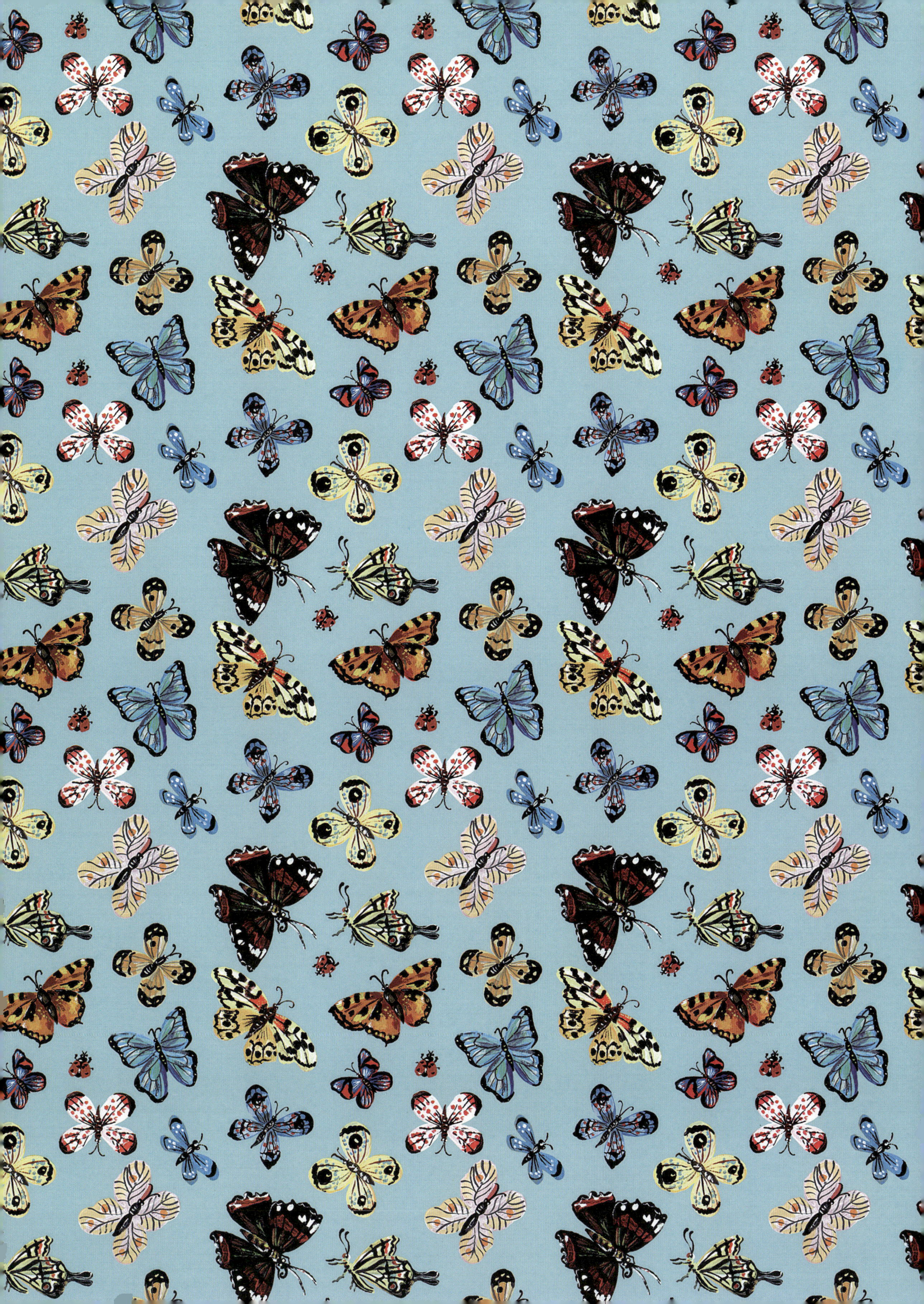

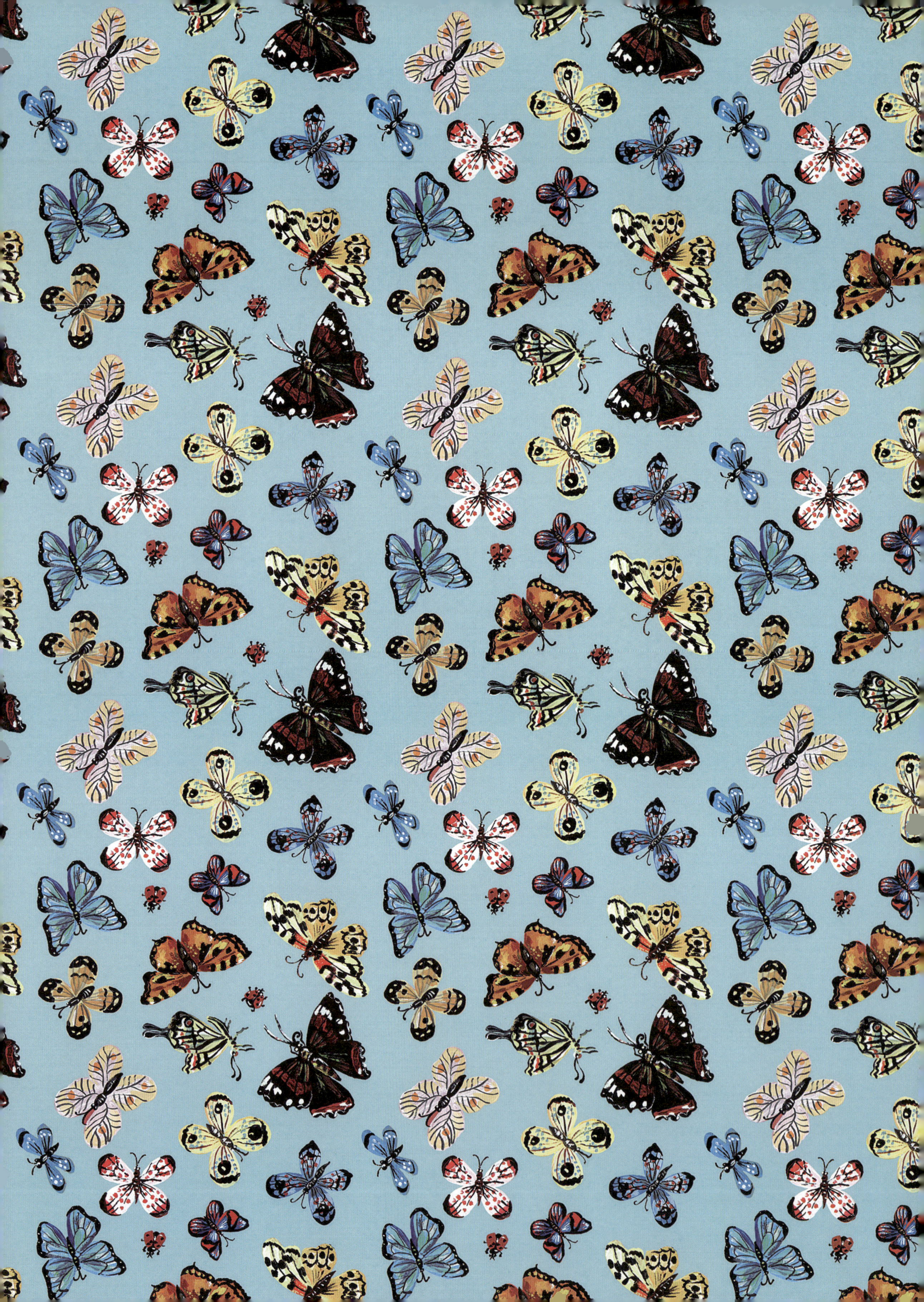

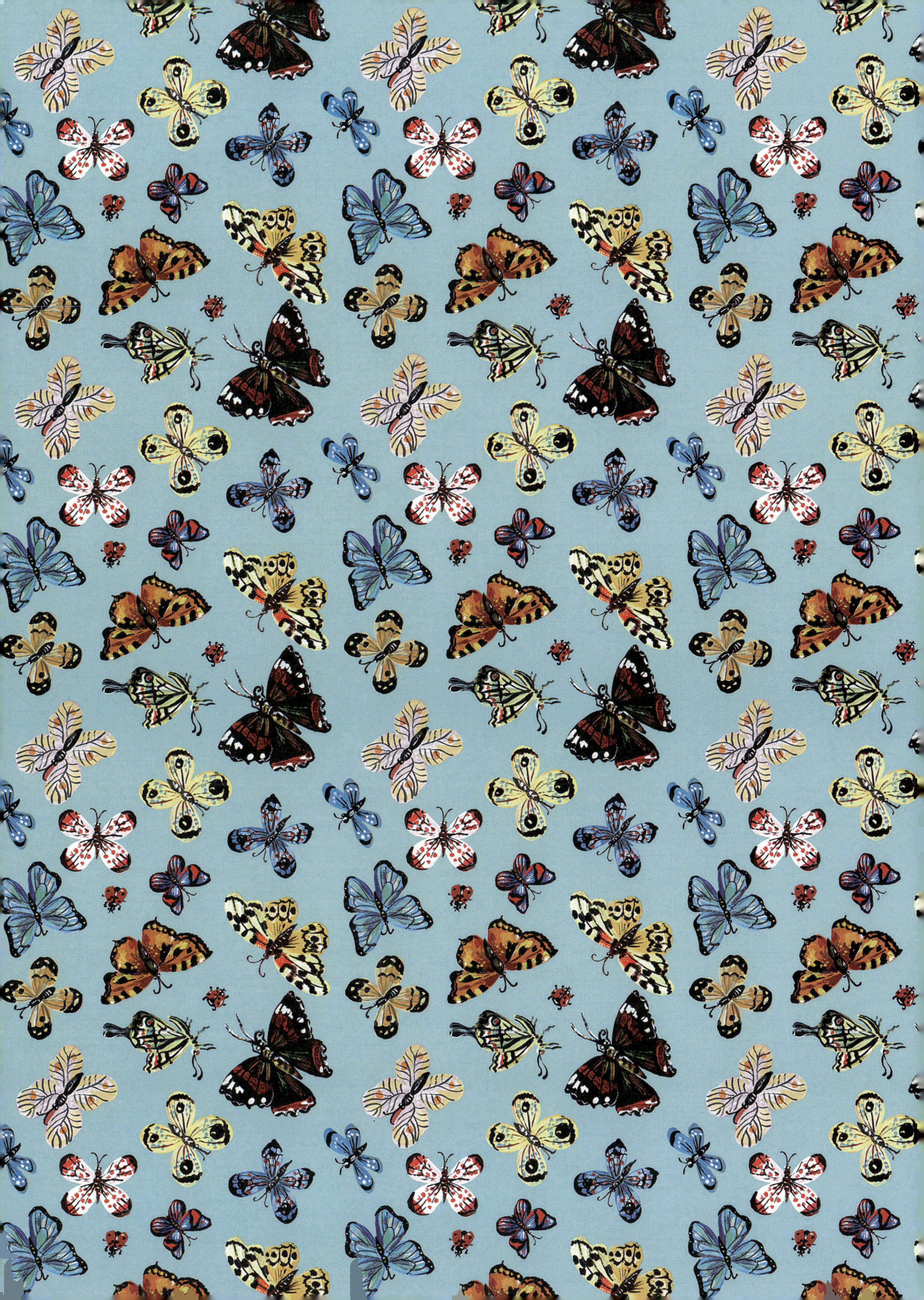

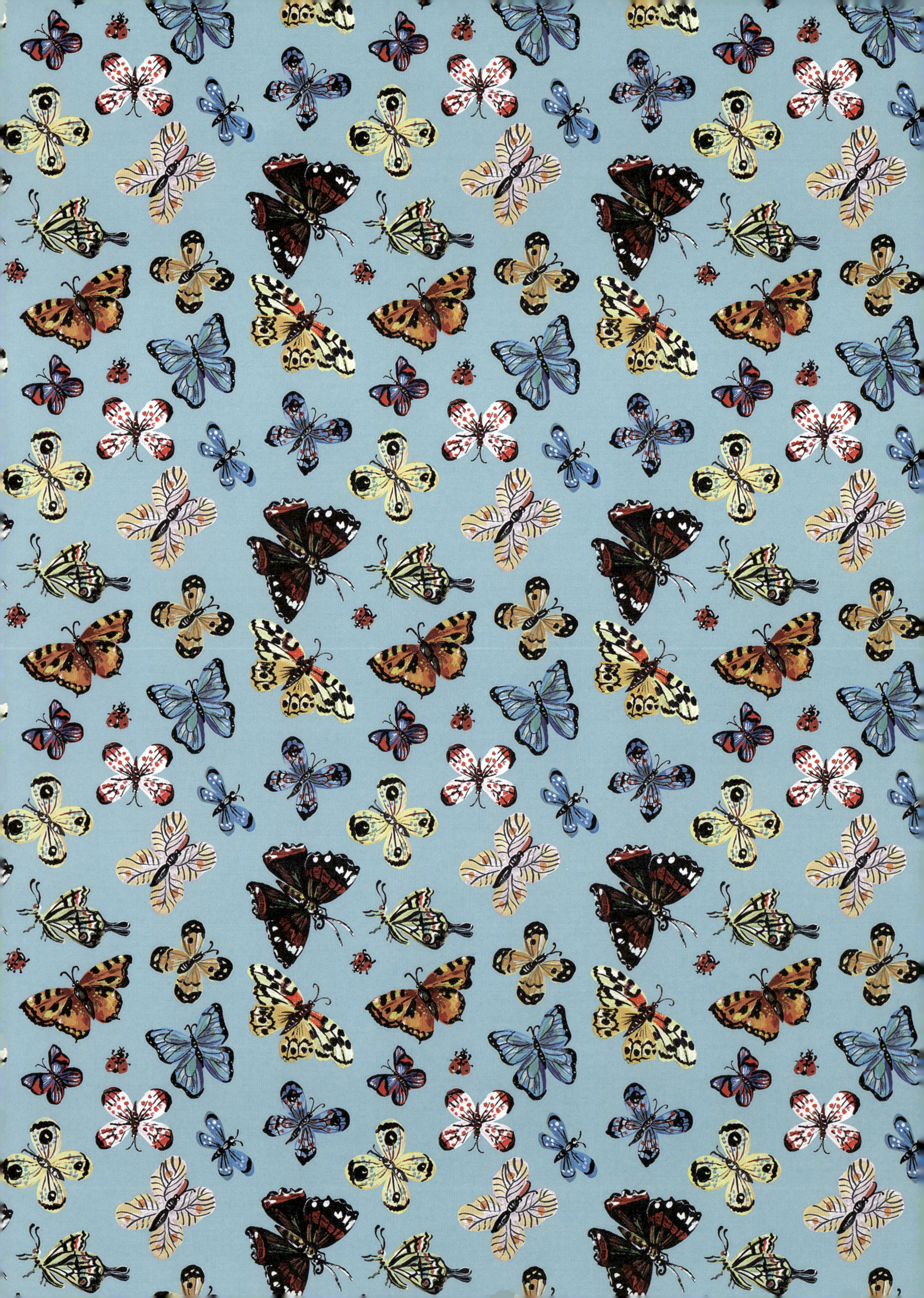

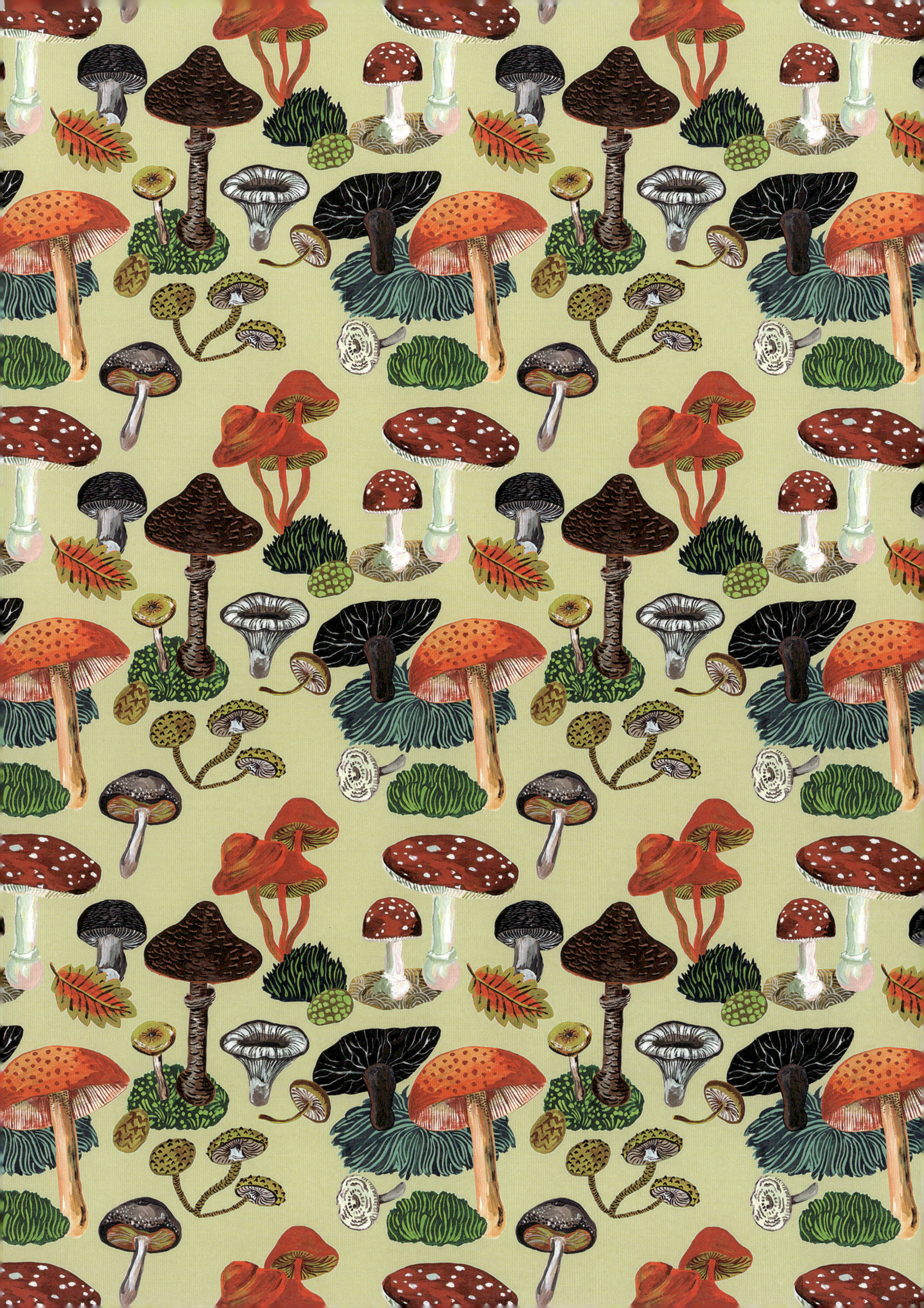

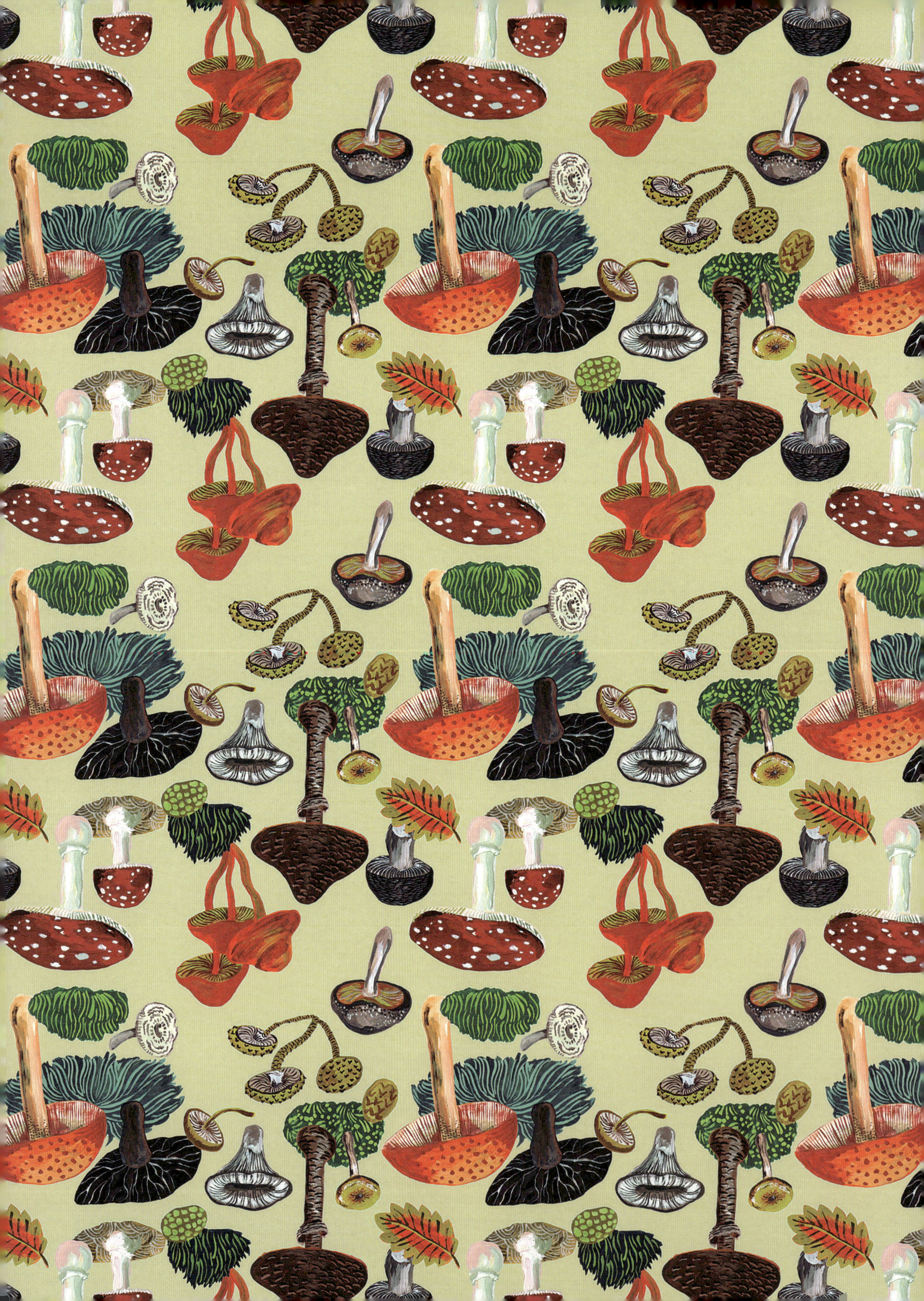

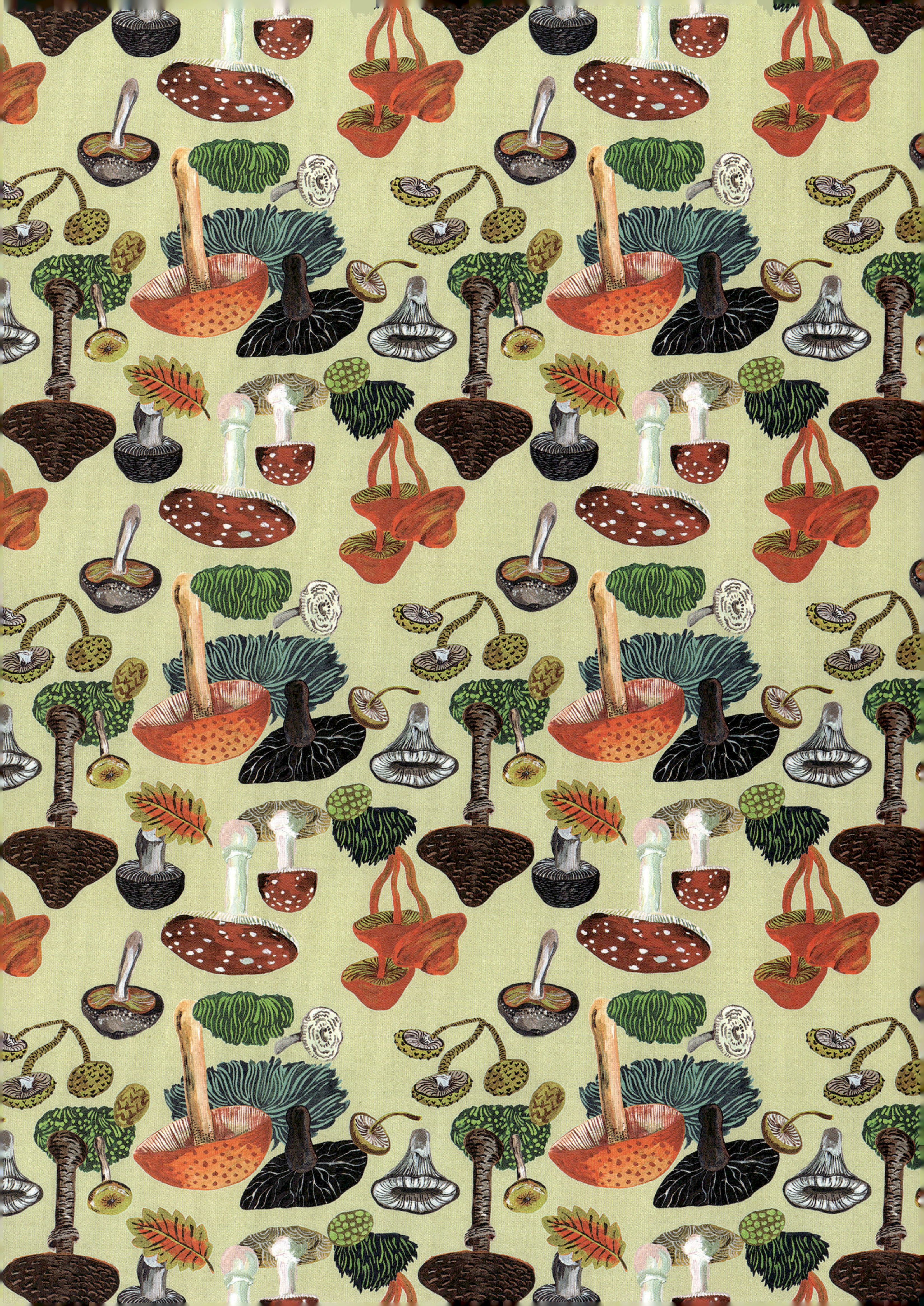

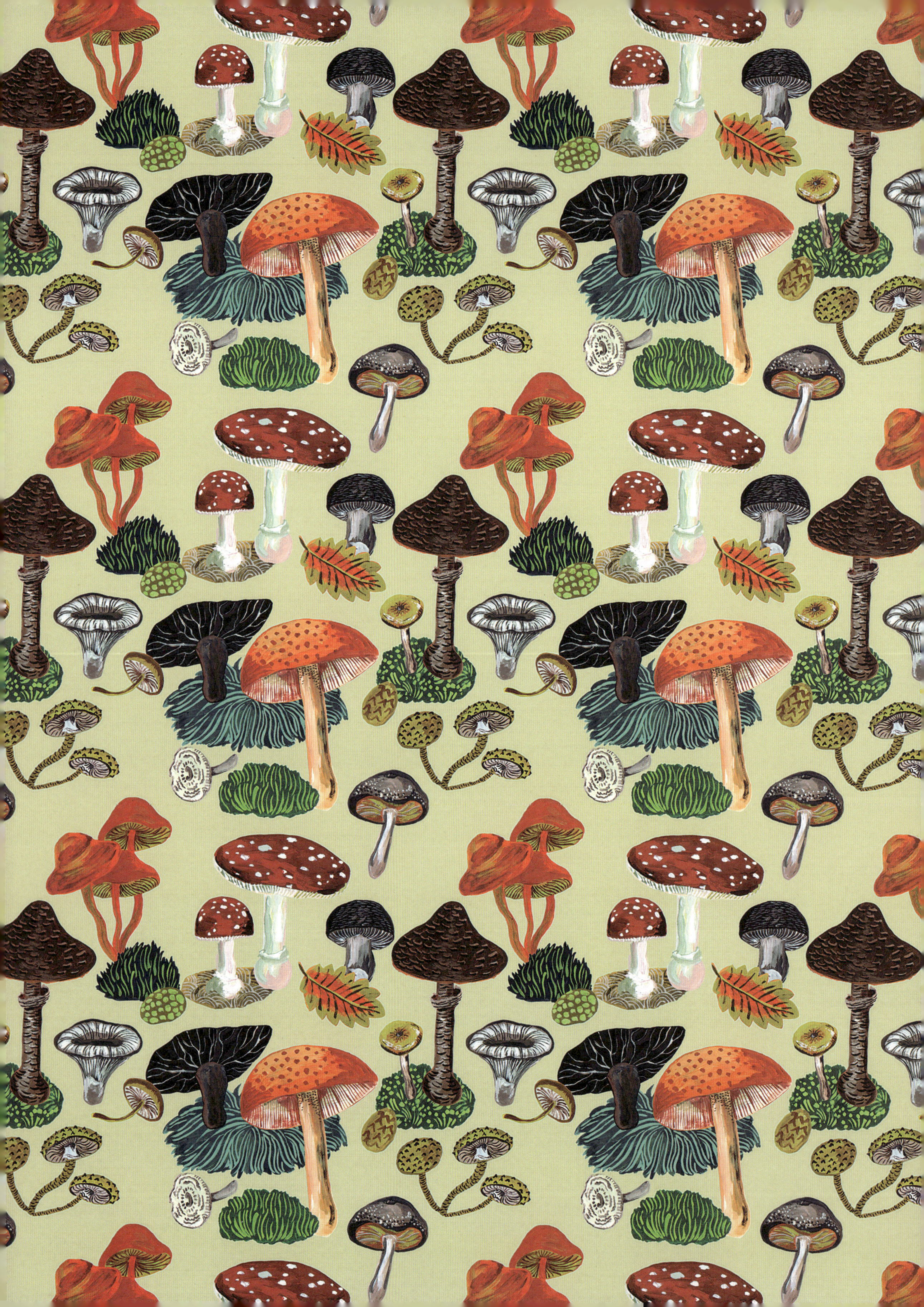

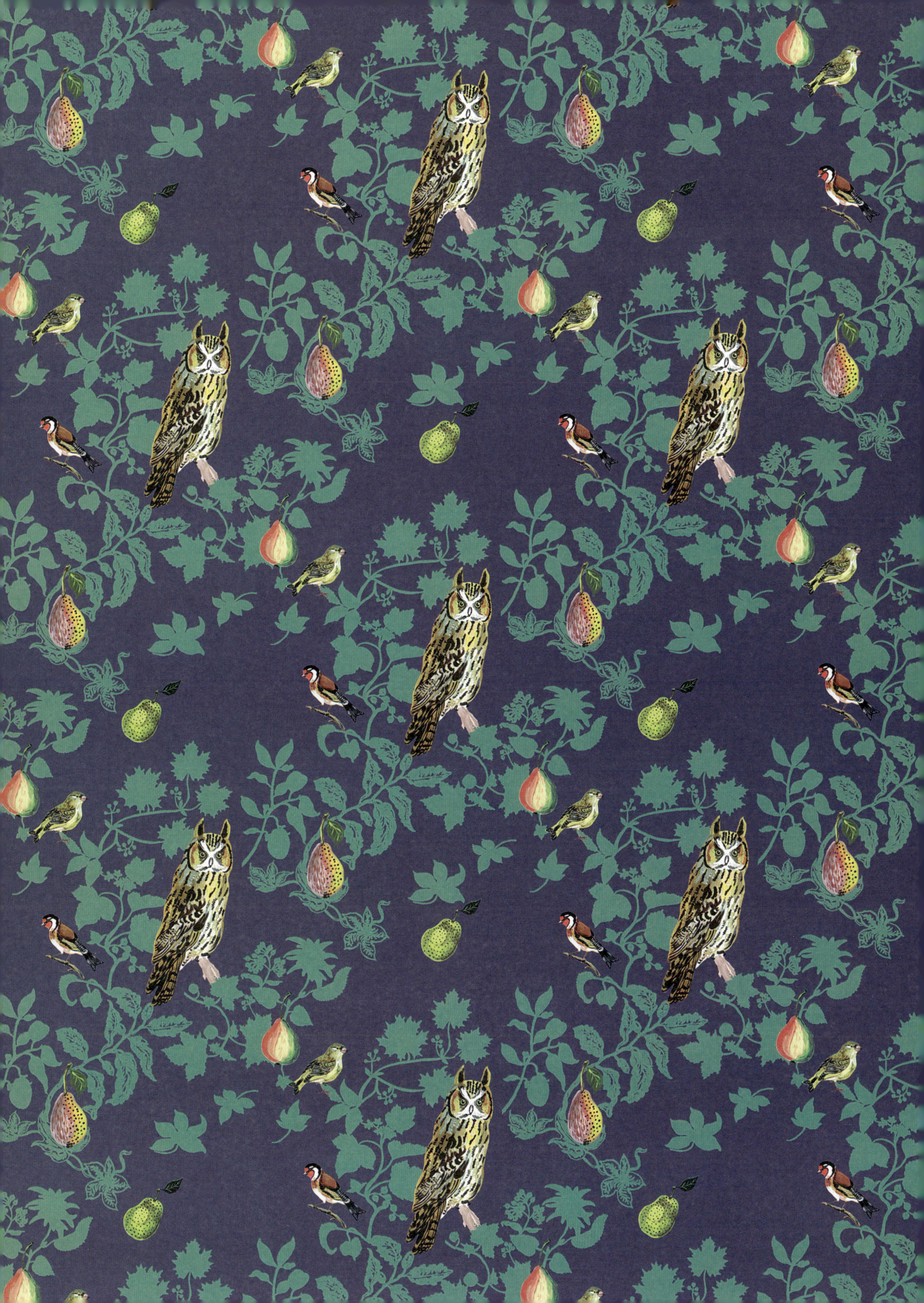

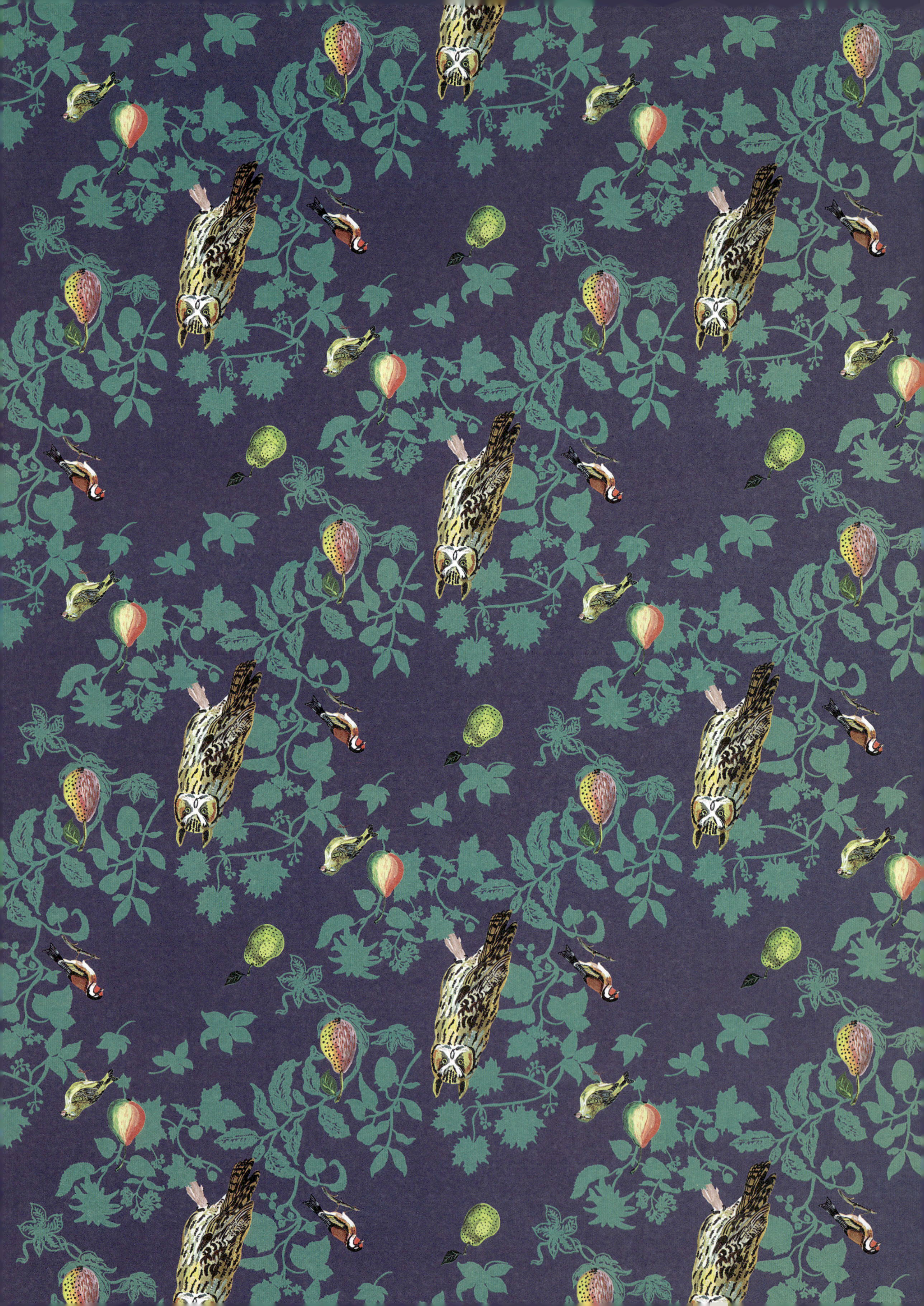

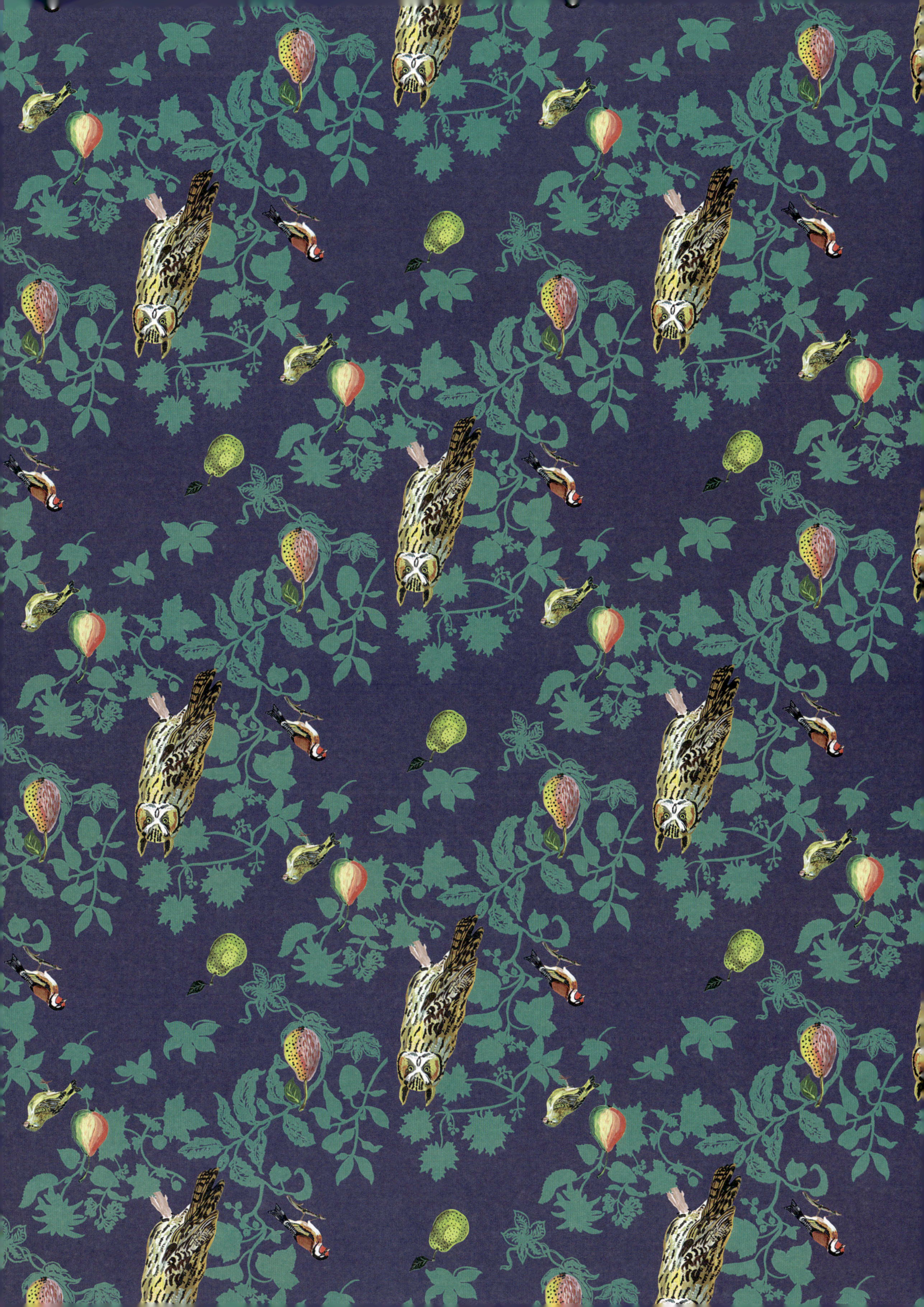

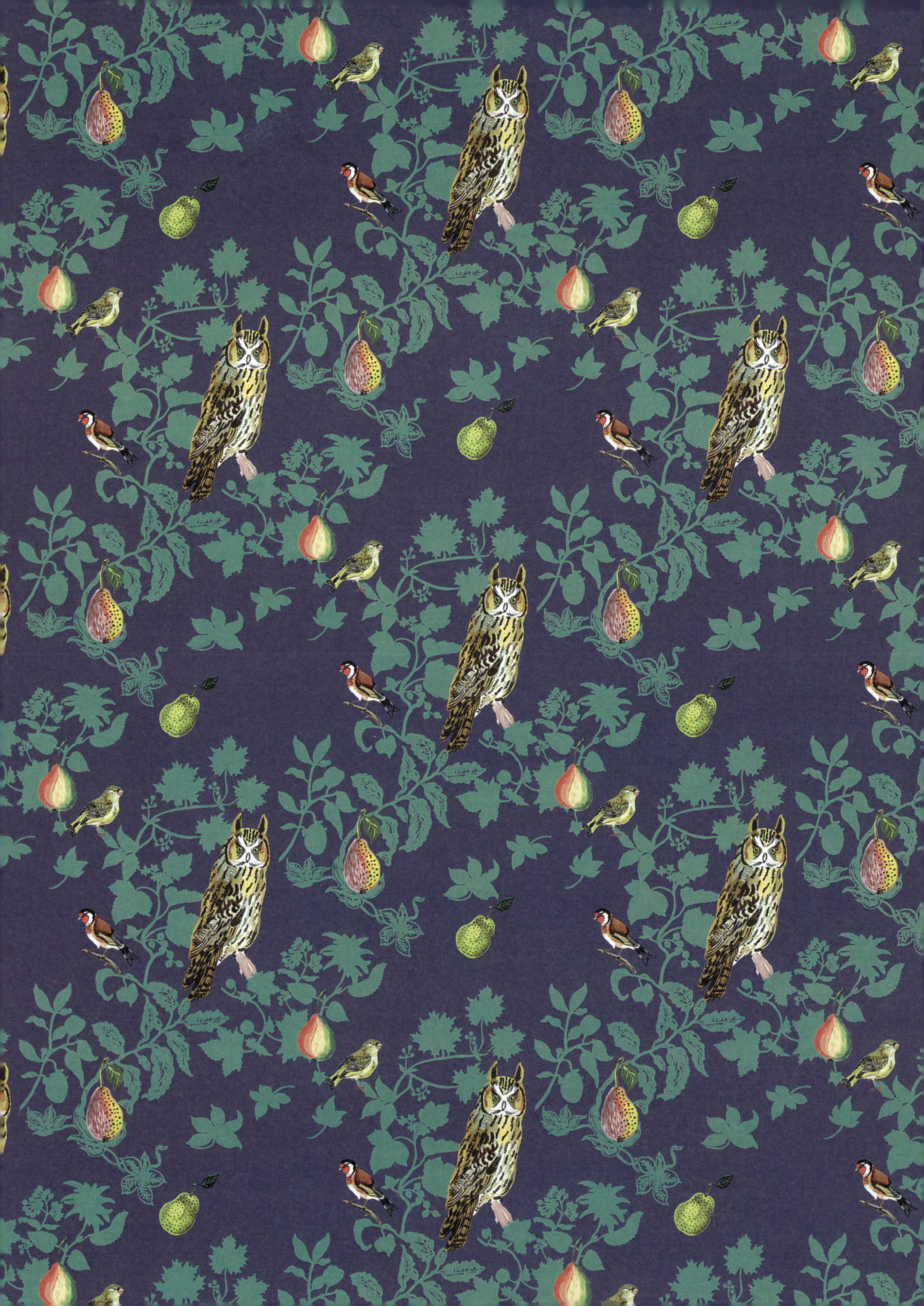

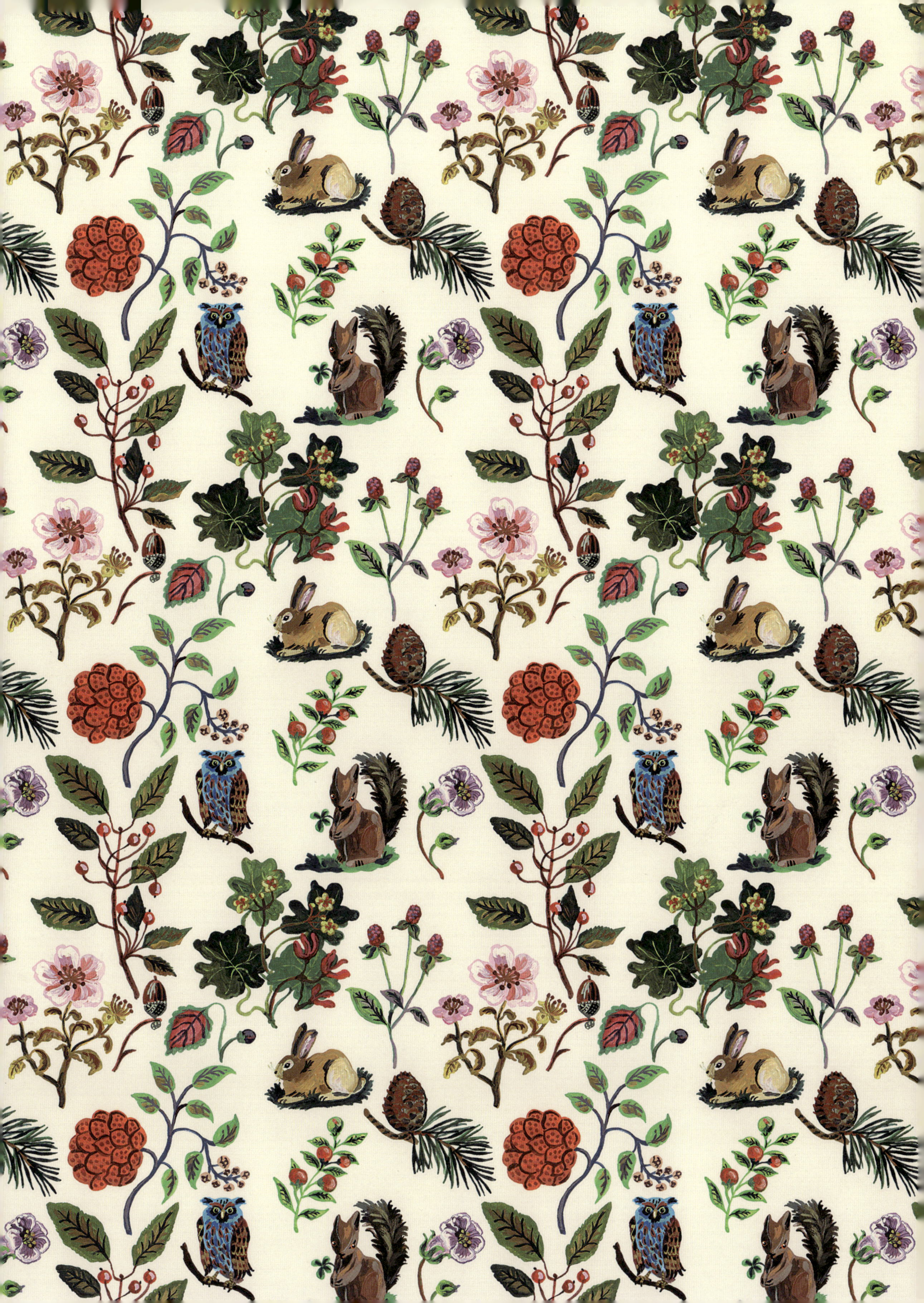

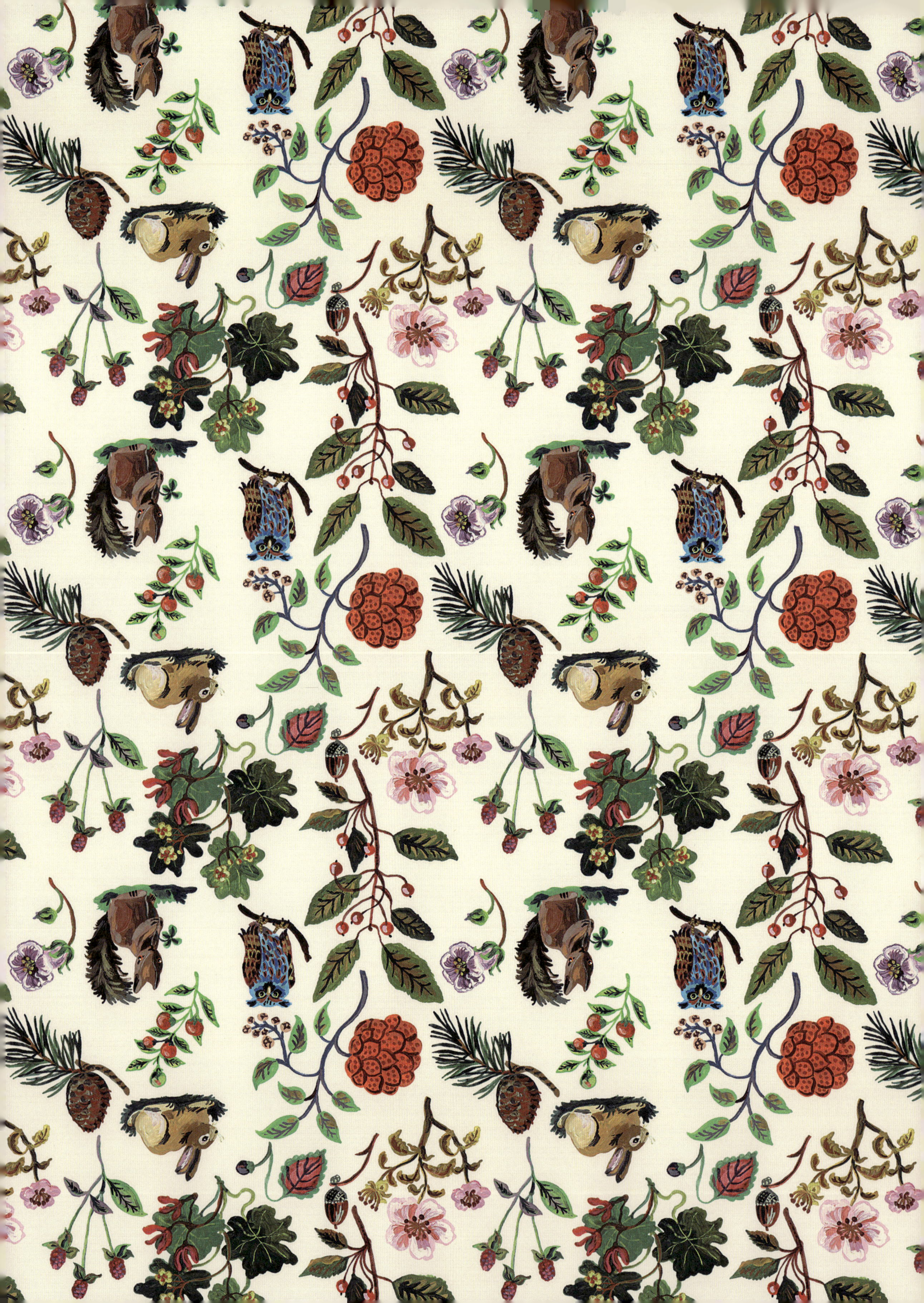

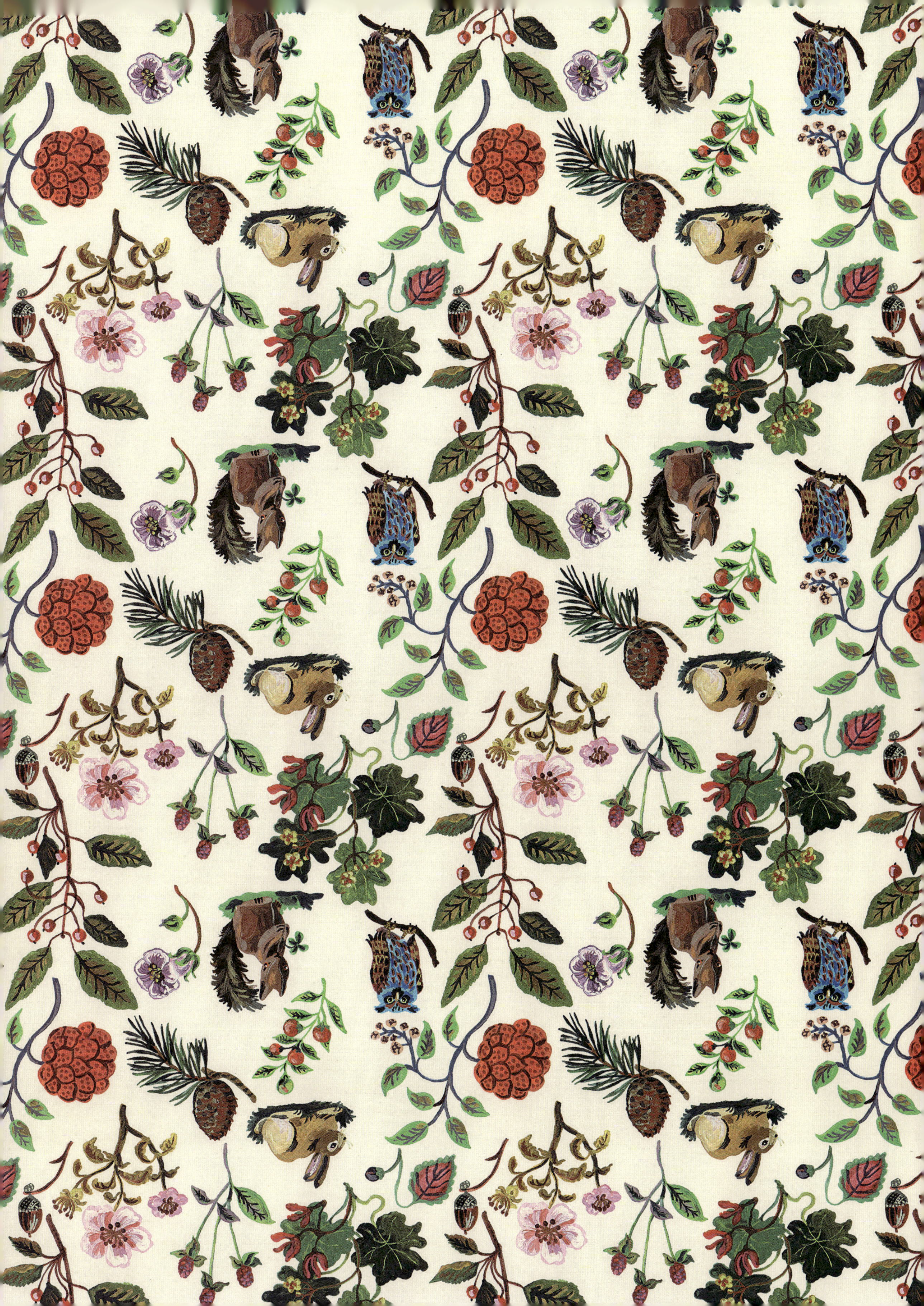

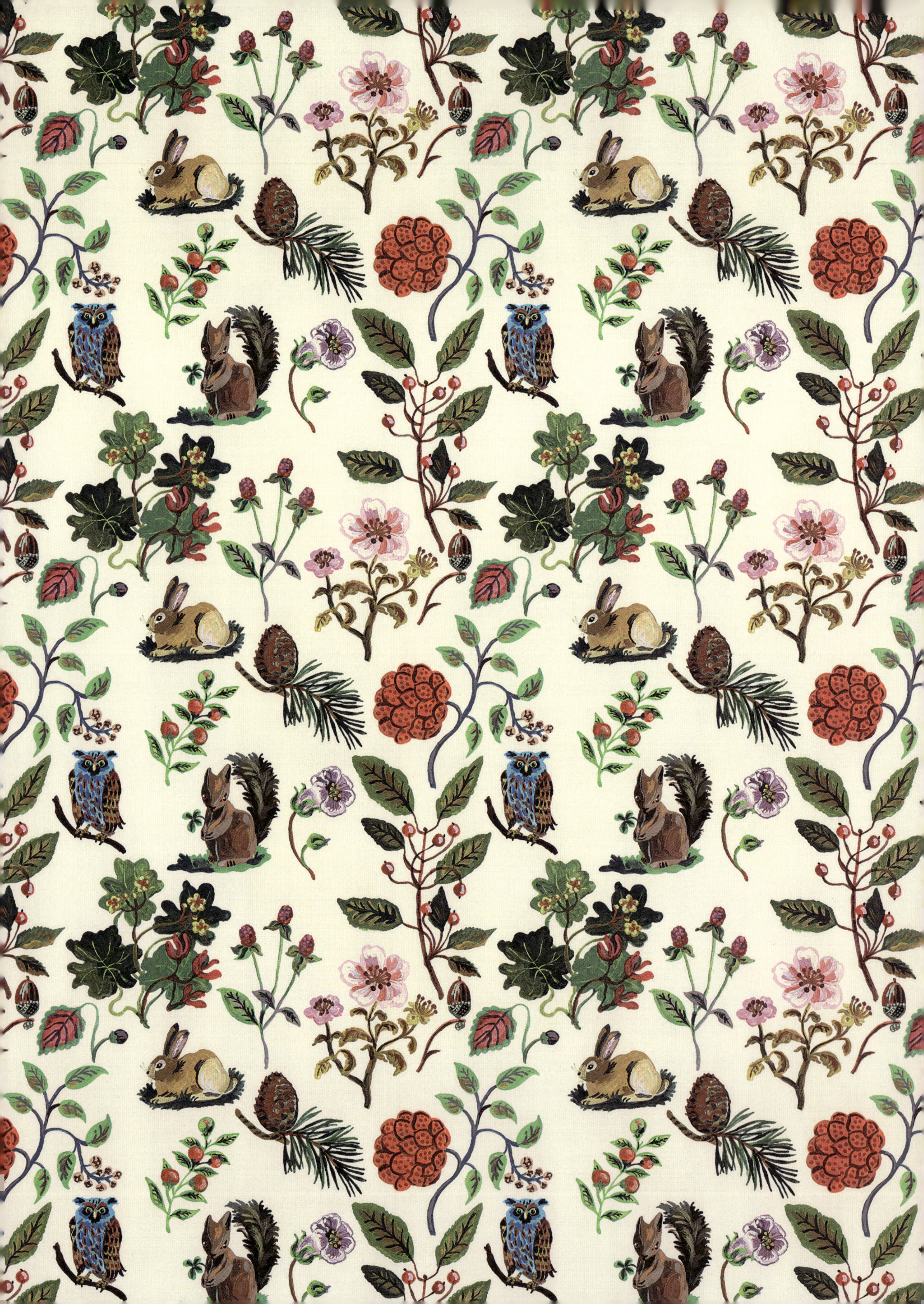

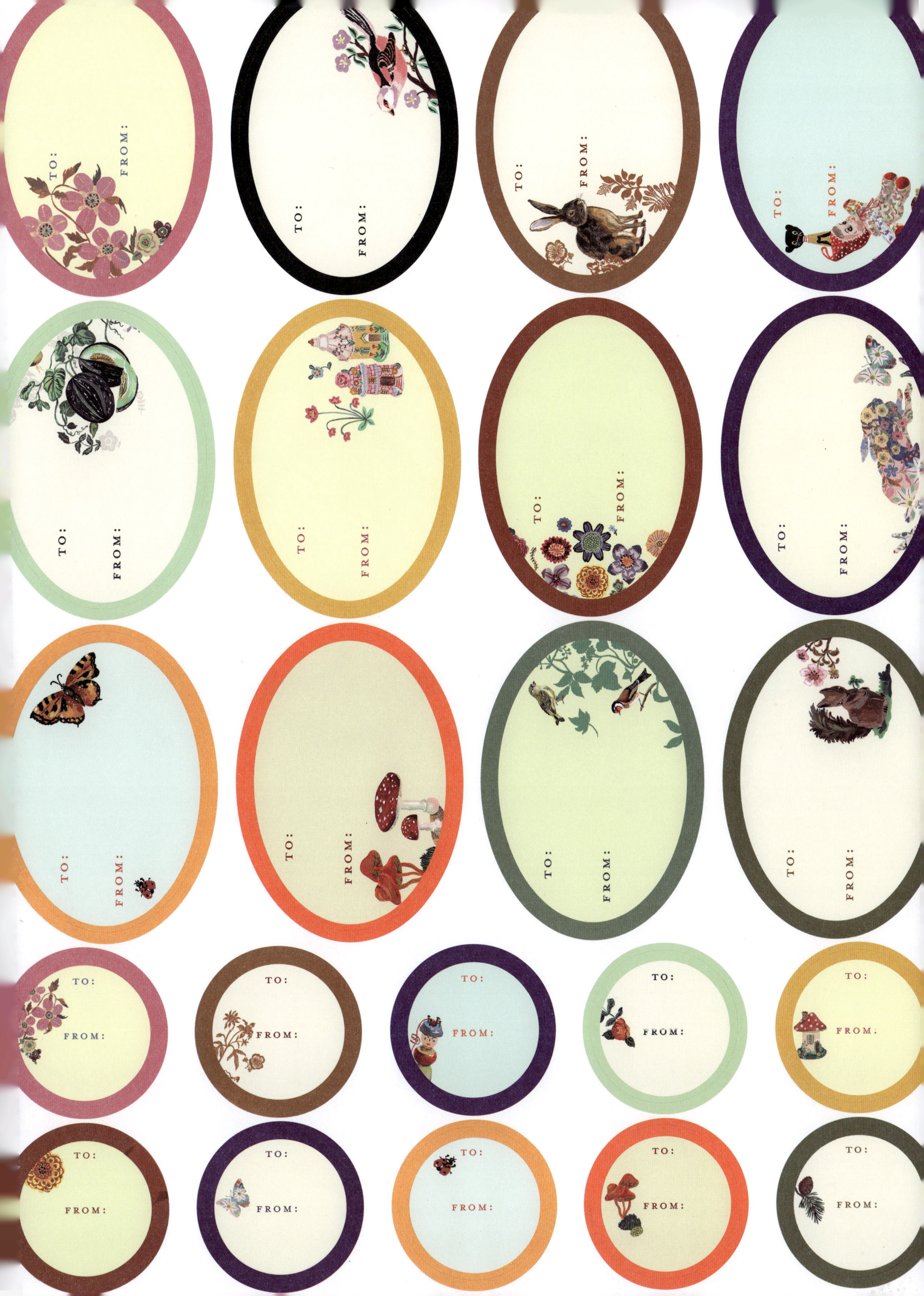

TO:
FROM:
TO:
FROM:
TO:
FROM:
TO:
FROM:
TO:
FROM:
TO:
FROM:
TO:
FROM:
TO:
FROM:
TO:
FROM:
TO:
FROM:
TO:
FROM:
TO:
FROM:
TO:
FROM:
TO:
FROM:
TO:
FROM:
TO:
FROM:
TO:
FROM:
TO:
FROM:
TO:
FROM:
TO:
FROM:
TO:
FROM:
TO:
FROM: